Being the Boss

The Power of Subsidiarity for Getting Things Done

Ian Wilders and Joan Kingsland

En Route Books and Media, LLC
Saint Louis, MO

En Route Books and Media, LLC

5705 Rhodes Avenue

St. Louis, MO 63109

Contact us at **contact@enroutebooksandmedia.com**

Cover Credit: The entrance of the offices in Spain shows a chess pawn where the shadow is a king. It was designed by Amandine Wilders to convey the idea of subsidiarity. It suggests that every person who acts as a pawn in the company's mission is someone who possesses the power and responsibility of a king in their own individual mission.

Copyright 2023 ExNarrative Ltd.

ISBN-13: 979-8-88870-078-5

Library of Congress Control Number: 2023944825

All rights reserved. No part of this book may be reproduced, stored in a retrieval system, or transmitted in any form, or by any means, electronic, mechanical, photocopying, or otherwise, without the prior written permission of the author.

Table of Contents

Foreword v

Introduction 1
   How it all Started 2
   Discovering the World 3
      Being Entrepreneur 3
      Travelling around the World 5
      Coming Back to Real Life 9
      The Group Falls on Hard Times 9
      Consulting 10
      Becoming CEO 11
      Starting with Clarity 11
      Implementing Subsidiarity 15

Chapter One: Management Tools of Subsidiarity and the Common Good 17
   Subsidiarity 17
   Aligning Decision-Making with Authority 18
   How We Introduce Subsidiarity to our New Employees 19
   Mission and Authority 22
   Spelling Out Personal Missions 24
   Align Power with Mission 30
   Respecting the Right Channels in Subsidiarity 32
   The Role of Management in Subsidiarity 34

Monthly One-to-One Meetings 37
Subsidiarity Flourishes in an Environment of Shared Common
    Values 39
    The Value of Trust 40
    The Value of Autonomy 41
    The Value of Transparency 44
Values for Team Leaders 46
The Common Good as a Corollary to Subsidiarity 48
    Once the Value of Common Good Showed Up 50
    Challenges to Upholding the Common Good 51
Resilience 54
    Asking "Who Will Replace You?" 55
Conclusion 57

Chapter Two: Leaky Financial Systems vs. Subsidiarity 59
Leaky Practice Number One: Executives Relying on
    Questionable Data for Major Decisions 61
Leaky Practice number Two: Budgeting so as to Remain
    Relevant and Spending because it's in the Budget 63
Leaky Practice Number Three: Instigating Company Policies to
    Control Employees 66
A Financial Management System in Line with Subsidiarity 67
    Getting Rid of Signed Purchase Orders 68
    Simple Spreadsheets 69
    Moving on from Spreadsheets 73
Setting up Budgets in a Subsidiarity Framework 77

Table of Contents

    Conclusion 81

Chapter Three: The CEO in Subsidiarity 83
    What Falls to me as CEO 86
    Making Sure Things Happen 90
    Redesigning the Office Space 93
    Dedicating Time to Meet with Team Members 96
        Some Examples of One-to-One Meetings 97
    Understanding the World and Being on the Lookout 102
        Keeping the Big Picture 103
        Taking into Account Narrative Bubbles 104
        The Go Game 108
        Driving the Strategy of Diversification (a Significant Aspect of Resilience) 110
    Helping to Recruit the Right People 113
    The Captain of the Ship 122
    Conclusion 124

Chapter Four: Closing the Loop on Subsidiarity 127
    The Subsidiarity Litmus Test 127
    Planning a Subsidiarity Refresher course for the Entire Company 128
    Session 1: What is Subsidiarity? 130
        Part I: Spelling out Key Concepts 130
        Part II: The Importance of the Mission 133

Session 2: What to Expect when Working in a Group using Subsidiarity?.. 134
    Key Concepts to Spell Out 134

Session 3 - The Manager.. 137
    Part I: A Virtual Post-it Exercise 137
    Part II: What the Manager Should Do and Should Be. 138

Session 4 - The Company Culture for Subsidiarity to Thrive.. 139
    Part I: The Common Good to put Everything Together 139
    Part II: Group Work?... 140

The Result, Adjustment and the Fruits...................................... 142
Conclusion.. 145

Final Conclusion 147
    Conclusion Joan: Educating in Subsidiarity.......................... 147
    Conclusion Ian: It is Worth It.. 150

Foreword

IAN

During my first internship, my boss regularly looked tired and unhappy. That was partly because he worked late every evening. On one of those late nighters, he posed a question that has stuck with me throughout the years. He said that when you're starting out in the work world, you've got to put in long hours and show dedication. Your job is supposed to take first place. But then, once you're a CEO, you're suddenly supposed to have a balanced life, a stable family, and show discernment. He wondered whether that was even possible.

Now, nearly 30 years later, having become a CEO, I think I've found a satisfactory answer to that question. I have time for my family, which I put first. I put in a good day's work without overdoing it. Meanwhile the business is thriving and, in general, our employees are happy. I've written this book particularly for leaders, so that they can benefit from this experience. It's directed towards all those who have responsibility over teams of people, whether a small non-profit all the way to a flourishing multinational business.

JOAN

I first heard about Ian's innovative managerial style from his sister. Fascinated by her description, I invited him as a guest speaker to explain his approach to my students. He contacted me shortly afterwards to ask me for some advice about a book he had begun writing on the same theme. At first I was only going to give a little feedback, but it didn't take long before the book had become a common project between us.

I pipe up regularly throughout the book offering "best practises".

As a teacher/professor for the past 30 years I've been able to contribute pedagogical insight along with my writing skills to this book. I'm constantly trying to draw details from Ian that would bring insight to our readers. He likes to be challenged, and if he doesn't have an immediate answer to a question, he'll have one ready the next time we meet. My one complaint is that he tends to understate his achievements or not mention them at all. He didn't think to share with me that his company received the "Exemplary Practises in Social Responsibility" in December 2018, a sure sign that he's doing something right!

Another sign that he is on to something good comes from a letter written to Ian by a consulting firm in which they provide an assessment of his employees' view of the company. This letter manifests how much they are onboard with the organisation's mission and values.

Introduction

What sort of expertise and knowledge is required for a person to become a CEO and then flourish in his/her mission? My background is in business, with a specialisation in finance, so I have insight on how business is conducted, but I'm not an academic, I mainly draw on my experience. Some CEOs are great salesmen, others financial wizards, others still are experts in their industry. But how many are experts in every single one of the areas they need to influence? It seems evident to me that CEOs don't need to be experts in everything; however they ought to ensure that the people with the expertise in their area are the ones making the decisions appropriate to their mission.

Being a CEO is all about managing people. And people are exceptional. Each one of us has a unique profile of experience, education and talents. We've all faced challenges in our personal lives, taking decisions and living with the consequences, and this gives each one of us a unique perspective on life.

The role of a team leader is discovering this potential and knowing how to adapt it to the company. The company is there to create value for its clients, its shareholders and society. The employees could participate as mindless cogs in the machine but then would we not be missing out on their full potential? I believe that discovering that potential, and adapting it to the necessities, is the primary role of a CEO, and the greatest way to create value.

Over the years I have shared my experience with other CEOs, who were struggling under their workload, and wondered how I coped and was so available. I also spoke with non-profit leaders and youth leaders. I was invited to share my experience in seminars to promising young leaders and often was asked for a book about my experience and insights. That is what brought me to write things out.

Through this book I will share my experience with you of how I've employed two quite unique management tools to build up the company where I'm CEO. First and foremost there's subsidiarity and then the common good. You'll discover why I wished to use them in the first place, the challenges we had along the way, and the benefits of using such powerful tools.

You will also discover the benefits of these tools. For me, as a CEO, I am available for those who need me and have the freedom to keep a strategic mindset in a changing world, whilst being sure that the business is delivering its full potential. I can be confident that employees are striving to create value for the company with a negligible overhead for control. On the part of my employees, they have the satisfaction of being able to express their full potential and own their victories. They also grasp their impact in our endeavour. Ours is a culture of dedication and ownership of a common mission that delivers results.

How it all started

I've been the CEO of this group for the last six years. Previously, I had worked here for eleven years and then left with no intention of returning. I had done many things in the company, from finance and administration to international commercial development. During that time I lived in three different countries, saw most of the operations, knew everyone and wanted to do more. Our group had its own management style and was prudent in its development. I believed it needed more ambition. I tried influencing the general manager to adopt another style and to be more daring. It was a trying time given that I saw so much that could be done. The leadership had created real loyalty to the group, nevertheless, there was much talent left unexpressed for lack of a proper channel. I spoke with the general manager and then the board and tried getting more managers to voice their frustration. But it was all in vain. Finally I wrote to the CEO to explain in detail both the shortcomings and the potential which could be developed. He responded that all I wanted was to take his place. That's when I first realised that you can help a CEO only as long as you're aligned with his management style and his vision. So rather than creating tension in a company I highly respected, with people I appreciated and with great products, I preferred to leave for good. Anyways, I wanted to launch new projects and discover the world. In the meantime, I kept my position as advisor to the board composed of four founding partners.

Discovering the world

Being entrepreneur

When I left the company I started by assessing my savings to see what could be done. For most of my life I had wanted to be an entrepreneur, to set up a company and enjoy the freedom of unlimited growth. My wife, Anne, and I had been saving up to maybe buy a house one day. We decided that I could invest the money to launch a company instead.

At that time electric four-wheel scooters for elderly people were all the rage in the UK and the US. I set a deadline of 18 months to determine if it would be a viable business for me to offer these to the French market.

As an entrepreneur I discovered how I needed to do everything, from purchasing, to sales, to marketing, to accounting, mechanics and more, including hauling huge boxes in and out of my car. When I hired a young lady to help me with sales that meant I also had to look after human resources.

We had some nice successes, such as being the official sponsor of one of the biggest fairs in Paris, where we sold quite a few units. However, as my 18-month self-imposed deadline drew near, it became evident that I did not have a business which could support my family. Till then I had basically broken even. I therefore needed to shut down and look for other opportunities.

In all, this was a great training ground for my business sense. I walked away with very practical and vivid examples of all the expertise and effort that are needed for embarking on a business venture.

At that point our savings would permit us to survive another 15 months, meaning there was time for me to find a job. That was when I got to thinking about a book Anne had often read about a couple who had travelled with their four children around the world. After calculating that living in Paris, where our children went to a private bilingual school, would not cost more than travelling around the world, I shared this insight with my wife. She jumped on the idea. Travelling around the world with her whole family was a dream she had never thought would be possible. We had a new project which would also deeply influence our worldview.

Travelling around the world

First we asked our children aged 14, 12, 10 and 7 if they would be willing to go. Had any of the three eldest been against it we would not have gone. They had to think about it and accepted on the condition that they would not lose their school year so they could keep up with their friends when they came back. That suited us fine.

As we would stop renting while we were gone, we started giving away what we didn't need and found a storage solution for what we would keep.

Anne went through the upcoming year's academic programs for our four children and stored all the material we would need for every subject, ranging from math, physics, history, French, Spanish , English and Latin. She stored everything on a trusted USB key, (making a copy of course).

We had three months to sort everything out, hand back our flat, and off we went. We left on the 15th of July 2008 and arrived back on the 14th of July 2009. Offering the details of this wonderful trip would take another book, but I would like to share a few organisational insights.

Managing the budget

Once the plane tickets were bought we had a budget of 130 euros on average per day. We would be traveling in about 10 countries: for each of these I made an adjustment according to the living standards and fixed the daily budget for that country.

We had a little notebook to account for all our expenses and calculate the surplus or overspending of the day. That would allow us to know how much we had for the following day and be able to continue our trip within our limited budget till the end of our adventure.

From the outset we entrusted this task to one of the children who took care of the accounting the entire time we were in one country. Then one of the siblings would take over in the next country.

It was wonderful to see how seriously they took their responsibility. Every time we would pay for something they made sure to keep track, whether it was renting a room, buying some food or paying a bus fare. Even when I had a beer, they would inquire about the price and duly write it down.

They also took the initiative to propose savings so we could spend more elsewhere. For instance, when we were in Australia, we wanted to visit the Great Barrier Reef. It would take a big toll on our budget, but if we could sleep in our rental car this would be possible.

Seeing how the children benefited from this exercise would later provide real insights for my professional life.

Our house in our bags

We had decided early on that we would be travelling by plane, bus, car or whatever we could. This meant that each one of us had to be able to carry all we needed in a couple of bags. Anne has great organisational skills, and suggested the items we would need such as shoes, sleeping bags, trousers and the few practical things we would use to survive. Each one of us was responsible for our own bag. We each needed to organise our own self as as we saw fit, including unpacking when we stayed over somewhere, and then making sure that we had everything when we left.

Soon, we all became experts in our own way. Our youngest daughter had a very special responsibility. Whenever we would leave a place, whether a youth hostel, a rented flat, a friends room, she would go around, slip under the beds, open the cupboards, explore the bathroom and check that no one had left anything behind. She would sometimes come back with a toothbrush or some underwear that had slipped through the cracks. Thus we had responsibility as well as quality control. For me this would provide another great insight in the professional setting.

Studying on the road

Since our trip started in South Africa during our summer holidays, we waited till September to start home-schooling. By then we were in Hong-Kong and I had spotted the notebook computers we needed. They were very light and cheap, meaning one for each child fit within our budget. Our children now had the responsibility of taking care of their computers.

We had decided that the younger children would have to study two hours a day while the eldest would need to dedicate three. They would study in motels, on buses, or wherever possible. Sundays would always be free. Anne and I split the subjects. I would take the sciences and Anne would look after all the others, meaning the three modern languages plus Latin. It turned out that we just needed to point out the course to follow and then our children would whizz through their work, just stopping on the more challenging points. When we had the internet, they would find the solutions online and move on. It was fascinating to see each one advance at his own pace. The youngest was the one who needed more attention as she was not as comfortable reading. My wife and I also had our own styles when helping the children. All this flexibility and creativity would continue inspiring me many years later.

An inspiration for management

As time went by we all looked back to this family adventure as a special time when we got to know each other better, to trust one another and build a family history. The children today have all continued with higher education, and have gone to universities in the United Kingdom, Switzerland and the Netherlands. As students they all managed their budgets with the skills they practised while travelling and continue to do so in their professional lives. They benefited greatly from the expertise they developed in researching the information they needed to complement their learning. I witnessed first hand how responsibility given within a solid framework had long lasting effects in many areas. This was a strong influence on my future management style that we will explore in this book.

Coming back to real life

When we had finished our world travel I really needed to find a job because our savings were finally running out.

Jumping forward a few years, by 2012 I had a consulting company that worked with startups who were having financial difficulties. That was when I came back to consult for the company I had left so many years ago.

The group falls on hard times

In 2012 the group was experiencing major difficulties on account of the financial crisis of 2008 and 2009. Sales in Spain, which represented 15% of our turnover, were carried out solely through one distributor. That distributor not only went bankrupt but, in a desperate bid to save their business, they found a way to reclaim the last six months of sales we'd already received. Basically, they emptied out our bank account.

Our company fell into a deep crisis: it was debt-ridden and couldn't pay its employees.

The finance director, together with the general manager, did an extraordinary job negotiating further credit lines with our banks. At the same time the CEO asked the employees, on a voluntary basis, if they would accept pay cuts to save jobs. The great majority agreed. This showed not only their solidarity with their fellow employees, but also how they had grown in respect for the management over the years.

Consulting

I'd been consulted about the crisis on account of my board position. It turned out that one of the initial shareholders was ready to grant a short term loan, but very wisely, and quite understandably had set some conditions. He would lend the money only if we believed that there were good chances of success. He said that if we had arrived at the end of the adventure it would be better not to throw good money after bad. He was ready to provide some help only if there was a real chance of success, otherwise he preferred to lose his initial investment.

I offered to do an audit of the situation. That gave me the opportunity to see my former colleagues again and to rediscover the day-to-day work of the company. I interviewed doctors, researchers, communication specialists, pharmacists and all the experts who form part of our company.

It quickly became apparent to me that there was a huge potential just waiting to be expressed. I found that my former colleagues were proud of the company they were working in, but sometimes frustrated by their lack of opportunity to channel personal initiatives that could help save the company. Over the next two months, in that desperate financial situation, we explored what could be done with the management team.

Becoming CEO

I presented the conclusions and the recommendations at the next board meeting. They were intrigued by the analysis. As the current CEO had just reached the legal age of retirement, the board asked me if I would be willing to take over the general management of the group and implement the solution I had recommended. They argued that I knew the company well, I knew the fundamental philosophy of the founders, and that I would be their best choice to carry out the proposed plan. I accepted and, on the basis of the plan, we got the loan.

That's how I ended up returning to the company I thought I'd left for good. In July 2013, there were 80 employees in Spain, Belgium, France and Italy. The current CEO was to step down at the end of December, so I had six months to get to know the company again, transfer authority, and start implementing our restructuration, before taking over as group CEO on the 1st of January 2014.

Starting with clarity

My first step was to define a clear organisation chart. Until then, it was always a little bit uncertain who did what.

When they saw the changes about to take place, and how this challenged their way of working and their unofficial areas of influence, some people preferred to resign and seek a new adventure. Unfortunately, I also had to terminate some positions that were not relevant in a struggling company. It was hard to see people go. In all, seven people left, nearly 10% of our workforce. The reduced salaries that the employees had accepted during the previous year were maintained.

Thanks to the loan, we were able to meet our financial commitments and concentrate on our business.

Best Practice: Clarity

Right from the start Ian strove to spell out the positions of authority as well as each person's specific role in the company. His organisational chart includes every person. It's a concise, objective format that provides for a clear and common understanding throughout the company.

So to get things going in your organisation establish:

- *Who has the authority.*
- *The specific role of each person in your organisation*
- *A clear organisational chart.*

Finding my management style

The current CEO and I had different styles. He saw his responsibility to be there to help, to guide and to make decisions. Accordingly, he was present in most meetings whether production, research, business development or others. On the other hand, I was not comfortable being in all the meetings as I was not an expert in the subjects being discussed. At the CEO's suggestion, I ended up attending some meetings, but I was only there to listen and understand. I didn't see it as my responsibility to make decisions.

In the month of November 2013, as part of my preparations to assume my new position in the company, I organised an offsite meeting with my direct management team.

The six of us went to Paris, with a consultant I knew, to explore subsidiarity, a management technique I'd discovered over the years. I had the intuition that this tool, if properly applied to a company, could deliver results. I was confident that an organisation principle which had stood the test of time could be resilient and efficient and more reliable than new management fads which come and go.

I asked them: "As a CEO, what do you want me to do in the company?" The previous CEO, who had a lot of experience, had been close to the action, was there for everyone, knew what each person in their teams was doing, encouraged them, and spoke to them about their challenges and successes. I asked if that is what they expected of me? Instead they politely but firmly suggested that I let them do their jobs and not meddle with their teams. I understood they wanted me to keep out of their day-to-day work. They were happy for me to be present for them, but not for their teams.

The consultant spelled out what this request would mean for me: asking employees about their work implicitly transmits a mixed message about who is in charge. It conveys the idea that the CEO can trump any decision and that the manager is not really necessary. I appreciated the wisdom of the request and was relieved. It wasn't my style anyway and it would have been very time-consuming and taxing to be ever-present for everyone. More importantly it showed that my management team was ready to explore and embrace subsidiarity!

Best Practice: listen first

Note how early on Ian ran an input session with his management team where he was there to listen. He dedicated time and money to the occasion. The offsite choice helped give importance to the meeting as well as focus. No doubt, the presence of an external consultant was important for establishing an atmosphere where members of the team would feel encouraged to be candid. The fact that Ian then respected the requests of his team to be hands off sent the message that their input was valuable. No doubt, this encounter contributed to building a relationship of trust and respect between him and members of his core team.

So to get things going in your organisation:

- *Find your allies within your organisation*
- *Dedicate time to work on the organisation.*
- *Organise a proper environment in which people feel their points of view are welcome.*
- *Encourage buy-in and feedback from your close team.*

Implementing subsidiarity

We implemented subsidiarity by the end of 2013. If you are reading this book, then you and I share something in common. We both have projects which we want to develop. And to do that we have teams of people to organise. The question is what is the best organisation for you? It is my contention that you can get more done by being many rather than being alone. That way you can get things done on a greater scale.

I had a team of 73 people, each with specific talents and experience. They were stretched over four different countries and knew the business better than I did. My ambition was to tap into all their potential.

If you've studied management styles, or if you search on the Internet, you know that there are many ways of organising a group of people. From autocratic to democratic, going through all shades of involvement. Nowadays, new management trends abound. Over the years, we've heard of empowerment and other ideas which sound very promising. But when implemented, the best ideas have their flaws and some can be fatal. We get into absurd situations when the vocabulary of what we do changes every few years just to comply with what is in vogue.

I was interested in a management style which had been proven by time. Subsidiarity met that requirement since it has already existed for almost 2400 years. It was more of a political approach, however, it could be adapted to any human organisation, not just that of the city. That's where this book comes in. I'd like you to experience how subsidiarity can work wonders within a company or a group of people sharing a common goal.

First, I'm going to explain what subsidiarity is all about. We'll then see how it spells out in practice. Next, we'll consider the specific implications for the role of the CEO in a company using the management tool of subsidiarity. Lastly we'll apply the pedagogical concept of "closing the loop" to round off the implementation of subsidiarity in a company. "Closing the loop" means circling back to ensure that all employees are working from a common understanding and acceptance of a given practice, in this case one that has become foundational.

Chapter One

Management Tools of Subsidiarity and the Common Good

Subsidiarity

Even as a kid I had inklings about the value of subsidiarity, though I never heard the word mentioned. At the hairdresser's, for instance, the logical thing to me would have been to let him cut my hair the way he thought best. But instead, I was required to say what I wanted while my mother threw in her opinion. End result: the same old haircut year after year. It seemed like such a waste of talent for the hairdresser. I was always left wondering, if he really knew me, what he might have done if only he had been given the leeway.

Then, there was my internal allergic reaction to my friend's insistence that I opine about all sorts of matters. If I didn't know the subject sufficiently, then I saw no use in giving my opinion.

I also really didn't like being told what to do. It didn't matter that I was just about to do a chore: if my mother asked me to do it, then my legs turned to sawdust. To this day, I still like owning my decisions and initiatives. So much for a taste of what brought me to use subsidiarity as a management tool.

I can't recall when the actual word subsidiarity came on my horizon. Maybe it was through an article or talk. Once you're aware of it, though, it seems to come up often.

Aligning decision-making with authority

I'm struck by two aspects of subsidiarity. The first is that subsidiarity puts decision making and authority on the front lines. People there really know first-hand what's going on and, furthermore, they have skin in the game. The second is that since subsidiarity has already been around for hundreds of years in the political and social arenas, it has something good to offer. Subsidiarity was already theorised by the Greek Philosopher, Aristotle, almost 2400 years ago and was developed by the great 13th-century thinker Thomas Aquinas. His thoughts were influential for one of the oldest international organisations in the world, the Catholic Church. Subsidiarity became central to the Social Doctrine of the Church.

At some point, I came to the understanding that if down through the centuries subsidiarity was so crucial for political organisation, then it could very well be a powerful tool in the business field. Admittedly, for a company facing difficulties and short on cash, subsidiarity was also a down-to-earth, inexpensive solution.

In 2013, I asked Jack, a consultant and trusted advisor of our company, if he would be up to the challenge of helping us explore the possibility of implementing subsidiarity in our organisation.

It turned out that Jack not only had a strong business and training background but being well versed in Greek and mediaeval thought, he also knew the principle of subsidiarity. So he was indeed able to offer guidance about the implications of exercising subsidiarity within a company, and was delighted to encounter someone who was ready to explore and implement this method at the management level. Jack warned us that this would redefine the concept of authority and my own role as CEO. It would not be anarchy or democracy but something else. We both knew that this adventure would make a profound impact on the company.

How we introduce subsidiarity to our new employees

Introducing subsidiarity to new employees is a fun, but challenging process. We try to help them see it in its historical perspective and political application before presenting what it looks like in a professional setting.

> ***Best Practice: taking a pedagogical approach***
> *In a very natural way Ian is taking the role of a teacher. One of his pedagogical moves is preparing the ground for learning to take place. Instead of jumping straight to the action that will be required, he's investing time to introduce the concept. Ian works from what they already know before moving to subsidiarity*

in the workplace. Another pedagogical move is following the natural order to learning: you need to understand something before you can begin relating it to other ideas. Being able to put a concept into practice comes still later. A pedagogical approach is important here because employees need to be convinced in both their minds and hearts of the value of subsidiarity if they are going to employ it well.

So in your organisation:

- *Be sure that you teach the approach to everyone in your organisation.*
- *Make sure they are on board.*

We start with a "Once upon a time": the ultimate decisions and responsibilities lay in the hands of the smallest unit of society, which for the ancient Greeks was the family. After a man and a woman were married, they had power over their own destinies and that of their children. Parents made the decision about whether their children would work or be educated. No authority could impose their will from the outside.

That didn't mean the parents stood on their own. In fact, they needed to count on others to fulfil their needs. For example, they were free to entrust the responsibility of educating their children to some outside person or school. Given that the parents had the responsibility in the first place, they could therefore entrust their power to carry it out.

The school, by the will of the parents, would be endowed with the power and responsibility for educating, meaning that the school could take the decisions needed to fulfil their education purpose.

For their part, the school might have felt capable of educating children, except in the area of developing a curriculum. Therefore, while remaining within their mission of educating children, they could entrust part of their responsibilities to another level which would develop the curriculum for them. When many schools entrust their responsibility to the same group, they create a regional academia. We see here how the mandate comes from the parents and is entrusted all the way through society to where there is most competence.

Another example of subsidiarity in society is security. A family may feel relatively safe in their house and neighbourhood. They're able to lock their doors and maintain a peaceful relationship with their neighbours. Nevertheless, a group of homeowners may feel insufficiently prepared to face dangers coming from outside the neighbourhood. Uniting together, they can entrust their responsibility for security to a specific organisation that keeps the neighbourhood safe. In their turn, this local police may feel confident in their ability to defend the area, but if some greater threat were to come from a neighbouring region, they know they would be overwhelmed. So they can delegate part of their responsibility to a regional organisation which could organise some sort of army.

Now this army may be well-trained, have the proper resources and skillset to set up a good defence, but nevertheless be incapable of facing too big a threat from a neighbouring nation. Regional armies can therefore delegate part of their responsibility and power to a national level.

The idea of subsidiarity is that power and decision start at the basic level of the family, but can expand all through society. Power doesn't originate from the head of a state and then trickles down to individual members. It comes from the base, with power and responsibility being entrusted to other levels of society as needed.

After speaking of subsidiarity in relation to the family and society, where the smallest units have full power and responsibility, we address the challenge of adapting this notion to a business organisation.

First of all, we draw the analogy that the person, each employee, is similar to the family in the previous society setting and is therefore central to the organisation. Those who best understand what's at stake in a given situation; those who have the most skin in the game are the ones who should have the power and the responsibility to make things happen.

Mission and authority

Let's pause here to address the question that immediately arises: "the power and responsibility to make what things happen?" In the case of political subsidiarity, a family makes choices in accordance with its dreams and aspirations; but in the case of a business setting, a company has a specific purpose. We therefore saw the need for an alignment, to make sure that the dreams and aspirations of each person would contribute to the company's purpose or, as we say, mission. Each individual within the company has a mission. Together with everyone else's missions, they contribute to achieving the company's overall mission.

For the company as a whole, every employee should be able to recognize its purpose through a simple mission statement that can be recited off the top of their head. We have cohesion when all of us agree on what we're doing and why.

In the case of my company, for example, our mission is to make immunotherapy available to all health professionals for the sustainable good of their patients.

The WHY is the sustainable good of the patients. That is what motivates us.

And WHAT do we do? We make immunotherapy available to all health professionals.

A good mission looks simple, almost too obvious. Ours took a while to spell out satisfactorily. For a long time, we didn't know whether we were working for patients or for health professionals. We considered health professionals as a means to get to the patients; but we felt something was not quite right.

Through our current mission statement, we achieved satisfaction at the thought of the patients' sustainable good being the end goal, the reason for our action and health professionals being our partners, whom patients could trust. What patients really need are great professionals who understand them, know them, and devise the best solutions for each one. Simply by clarifying our mission, we found that everyone in the company could align their efforts.

In subsidiarity, the power of such a mission can provide the founding structure for the entire organisation.

Spelling out personal missions

Once the mission of the company is clear, it's possible for individuals within it to spell out their own specific mission. A person's mission lets them know their area of freedom within the organisation and how they are helping in fulfilling the company mission.

There are three characteristics to a mission.

1. It is short, so as to be easily memorised word by word.
2. It explains WHY the purpose is necessary and important.
3. It is an agreement on WHAT is going to be done. … and there is no HOW

The personal mission is an agreement between the person and the company stating WHY the person is there and the importance of their collaboration. It's an agreement of WHAT will be done to achieve the WHY.

For instance, the mission of Lucas (all names are fictional to protect the identity of the employees), the head of production, is to make sure that we always have the medicinal products in quantity and quality to answer demand at any time.

> The WHY is to answer demand at any time.
> The WHAT is to make sure we have what we need to comply with the WHY.

This is a very broad mission adapted to the personality of the head of production. He's responsible for estimating what the demand will be and for providing the needed resilience to make sure that unexpected events do not prevent him from achieving this constant availability.

The wording of his mission doesn't imply measurable production objectives as there are no predefined quantities to produce. We live in changing times. For instance, take the Coronavirus crisis. At first, demand spiked as patients were getting ready for lockdown; then demand dwindled as people were encouraged to stay home and away from all shops, pharmacies included. Lucas knows his mission grants him the full power and responsibility to take necessary measures as long as he works within the constraints of his resources.

Best Practice: make sure everyone has their personal mission clear

The founding block of subsidiarity is the mission. A simple clear mission explains what is being done and why it is being done. The mission is agreed upon between the person and their boss. There is a commitment on both parts.

So in your organisation:

- *Define a mission for your organisation in simple enough terms for everyone to know and memorise.*
- *Make sure each person knows and owns their own mission, which needs to be aligned with the organisation's mission. Each person, with their direct manager, needs to be involved in spelling out that mission.*

Once the mission is agreed upon, the person has full responsibility and power to achieve the mission. Their manager will no longer have the responsibility for that mission.

Responsibility is a strong word. When something goes right, it's thanks to a particular person, and when something goes wrong, we know who can learn from it. First and foremost, responsibility means that any strategy, any means which are used, must be decided upon and adapted to reality by the person in charge of the mission.

Obviously, no one else can have the exact same responsibility. There's an area of freedom, of autonomy, where each person knows that they are free to do what's needed so that things actually happen.

Important value is created within a company precisely when people take the right initiatives at the right moment. By being close to the situation they can analyse the circumstances at any given moment, know what to do, have the power to take the necessary steps and do it.

For instance, the mission of Matthew, our head of maintenance, includes the responsibility of ensuring secure production and office spaces. He's aware of the habitual comings and goings of people to our facilities, as well as the relative risk of our neighbourhood. While Matthew has the ambition to stretch as much as possible, he's also conscious of the limited resources he has to fulfil his mission. He had been looking for security options and found the perfect solution at a great price during the summer, when I was off on holiday; but that didn't hold him back as he knew he had the power to negotiate, purchase and get the system installed. Every step clearly fell under his responsibility.

What a satisfaction for me to witness how free our employees are to seize good opportunities and act! When I came back from holiday, we had a new functional alarm system. Matthew made sure I had all the necessary authorisations and access codes. I didn't need to be there to make things happen: Matthew knew his mission and made it happen.

Another example is the production area. I only go there occasionally with VIP guests, because it's a restricted area requiring elaborate dressing and preparation procedures. Each time I do happen to go there, I'm happy to discover new machinery and infrastructure. All the decisions are being taken by the right people, not me. I'm not signing purchase orders or authorising projects. Thanks to the mission of our financial director, I have the confidence that everything stays within our available resources and that what needs to be done is happening without delay.

Then there's Fiona. Before I became CEO, she was head of what was called the marketing department. She had a vision of what should be done and how to go about it; but unfortunately she was simply told what to do. Though she had proposed a better way, she would follow orders and was unsatisfied by the impact of what she was doing with her team. Not surprisingly, her whole team was frustrated. When I analysed the company before coming back, she expressed that though she had the title, she didn't even think the company had a marketing department.

When the organisation was reshuffled for the sake of implementing subsidiarity, Fiona was made head of the new communications department. Her mission was to make sure that our ecosystem would understand what we were about, so that health professionals could integrate our therapy in their daily practice.

Fiona suddenly had wings. Though I knew she was a great professional, I wasn't aware of her full potential. Today, after a few years, she has succeeded in positioning us in the mind and heart of thousands of doctors in Europe and has provided the occasion for many authorities and officials to understand our importance in the ecosystem of health. Just moving out of the way, letting her express her potential, was the best way to success.

A final example for now is of Dr. George, whom I met while I was still in the analysis phase preceding subsidiarity. At that time, Dr. George wasn't up to much and certainly wasn't taking any initiatives in the company. I wondered why. It turned out that when he had started to work for us a few years back, he had a number of initiatives including a very ambitious way of showing how our therapy worked. He invited people from his network of friends and professional contacts to participate in this project and they were willing to do so without pay, because they were interested in their friend's enthusiasm and the novelty of the therapy. They wanted to help. Once Dr. George had everything ready he informed management, never suspecting that they would veto the project. In one single stroke, Dr. George lost his credibility with his network and became bitter and disillusioned. At least that's how he recalled the episode. No doubt the management had good reasons for their action; nevertheless, the lack of clarity on who could take decisions stole the company of initiatives and new ideas.

Best practice: create an environment that encourages initiatives!

Initiatives are very fragile. Like a flickering flame, they can be snuffed out easily. On the other hand, if a good initiative is given the chance to grow, it can multiply exponentially, changing the world.

So in your organisation:

- *Help your employees to connect the dots once they have their mission clear: they are not only free but are expected to come up with initiatives to respond to needs and opportunities that arise within their area of responsibility.*
- *Make sure that successes are linked back to those who take the initiatives.*

Align power with mission

Power is the ability to make decisions and carry through with them, even if they get challenged. Power involves the capacity to pay for things. If decisions can be taken, but payments need to be authorised, then we're back to square one. We all know the one paying is the one who calls the shots.

Clarity in the area of responsibility is a mighty tool unlocking potential, and allowing initiatives to flourish. Real responsibility, in fact, must come with power. Confusion reigns when people are told that they have the responsibility, but all decisions must be validated by management. Either management simply rubber stamps decisions or it decides whether or not ideas are accepted. In the latter case, the responsibility therefore belongs to management and not the person. Companies following subsidiarity must therefore avoid the need to give authorisation.

People have a specific responsibility as team leaders. They need to be free to organise their team as they see fit, and define with each team member their individual mission. Each team member, in turn, will have their own area of responsibility and power. The whole idea is to put power in their own hands, so they're able to express their potential.

> **Best practice: get rid of authorisations** (more about this in Chapter Two)

> You will see in the next chapter how transparency in the company will help ensure that employees make good decisions about the use they make of the resources entrusted to them. Our point here is that having the power to make purchasing decisions is a natural consequence of subsidiarity. It goes with a person's specific mission.

> So in your organisation:

- *Assign yearly spending amounts to each department head and have them do the same with their direct reports, etc.*
- *Explain why authorisations for purchases will no longer be needed, because each person holds the responsibility for financial decisions within their mission and financial limits.*
- *At first you may want to offer moral support to your direct reports about making financial decisions, but hold firm in not making the decisions for them.*

Respecting the right channels in subsidiarity

I heard of a CEO who assessed how his business was doing just by looking at how full the dustbins were. Even though we're taught to have key performance indicators, CEOs will develop a feeling for how their business is doing by considering subtle changes. For my part, I'm very interested in knowing if people enjoy their work and experience fulfilment in their lives, given that they're dedicating their time and energy to our mission.

I would love to ask employees about how they're doing, what they're up to, their challenges and solutions etc.; but I know that probing in such a way would be destructive to an organisation in subsidiarity. Most of the employees in the company are outside of my direct responsibility, so if I start asking them how their work is going, I'm sending the wrong message. I'd be transmitting that I don't trust their managers to share the right information; moreover, I'm thereby giving the employee the right to judge their boss on an ongoing basis.

I don't want to interfere with the work of my team members, so I try to keep out of their business. When I start chatting around the water fountain or over a coffee with an employee, we can talk about anything besides work. We'll talk about the weather, sports, local customs and culture, but I'm careful not to ask how their latest activity went, or what they're hoping to achieve. If they come back from a trip, we can talk about what they thought of the city, whether they had time to explore, but not about the purpose of the trip.

This is difficult for me as I'm really interested in what they're up to; but thanks to our practice of transparency, I can access all the information I need.

Through my informal discussions, I at least get a sense of the employees' attitudes and mood. If I do happen to perceive that something is off, I'll share my thoughts with their manager at an appropriate moment. This doesn't mean I'm unavailable to talk about work. Everyone knows they can send me a message to have a private meeting. If someone wishes to speak about their job, or even criticise their boss or understand what's going on, they can take the initiative to talk about it; however, I'll never take the initiative out of respect for my direct team and in coherence with the way we organise ourselves.

Best practice: keep your nose out

Ian would love to know what all his employees are up to, but he's aware that conversations about business with those who are not his direct reports could go sour. He needs to be very intentional therefore about what sorts of conversations he will have.

So in your organisation:

- *Watch that your conversations with employees do not get into the nitty gritty of the challenges of their work.*
- *Keep an open door policy to allow employees to reach out to you about whatever they want, but do not instigate such conversations that implicate their hierarchy. Establishing these parameters keeps coffee breaks etc. to lighter, friendly exchanges.*

The role of management in subsidiarity

At this point, some people will be wondering what's left to the management in a company such as ours? What exactly is the role of the hierarchy in a company using subsidiarity, when full power and responsibility are in the hands of the individual employees?

That employees get to decide what to do may sound alarming to some people, but in fact efficient leaders will give as much as they can of their responsibility and authority to their team members. Managers have their attention consumed by the responsibilities they actually keep for themselves, when instead they ought to be available for their team.

Here we can recall the analogous case of parents who possess full power and authority, but delegate some aspects of their responsibility to others.

A manager is important for individuating missions. When there's overlap, someone needs to be able to help clarify the situation and make things happen. On such occasions, a team member can ask their team leader for help and support.

Those in charge must also give the necessary followup to ensure that individual missions match both a person's potential and the company's mission. A mission should be adapted to a person's skills, experience and personality. Often the reason behind repeated failures is that the mission is not adapted to the person. If missions are poorly defined, there can be overlaps of responsibility and confusion, or some need gets overlooked and the manager loses time filling in the gaps.

Finding the right place for each person is an ongoing challenge for a manager, because there's a risk involved in entrusting a person with responsibility. If it turns out that they're not able to adapt, if they don't step up to the responsibilities, they'll also show signs of dissatisfaction and be harmful to our company. An adjustment is in order for both the good of the person and the company, but it might involve a demotion, which could be humiliating. All in all, managers need to be prudent and tactful in this aspect of their responsibility.

Managers define the strategy of their particular teams, similarly to how I define the strategy of the entire group by the organisation and the missions that are agreed upon with my direct team members. But strategy doesn't stop there. Each person, within their own mission, needs to develop their own strategy and tactics in their areas of influence.

The managers fulfil a crucial role in helping each person of their team to be strategic. An important tool for them is one-to-one meetings once a month. There, the manager will try to understand what is happening. Despite there being constant interaction at work, the overall picture isn't always clear. As we've already seen, initiatives can be taken without the manager being in the know, and that's fine. Nevertheless, the head of a group or section needs to have a good sense of what's going on, to ensure that everyone is able to participate in the overall mission and carry out their own ongoing mission.

> ***Best practice: follow up to make sure people have the right missions and that responsibilities are being covered adequately.***

If it's the mission of your direct reports then you need to provide the follow-up as regards making sure a particular mission is the right fit. If it's the mission of anyone else, then encourage the person in the correct line of authority to make this happen.
So in your organisation:

- *When there's an overlap, help set boundaries as to where the responsibility lies.*
- *When there's a gap and something is not being done or addressed properly, discern whether someone new is needed to meet that need or whether this responsibility can be fit into someone's existing mission.*
- *When someone is not adequately fulfilling their mission, consider adjusting that person's mission to something they are able to fulfil. Ramifications of that adjustment will be part of the consideration.*

Monthly one-to-one meetings

The monthly one-to-one meeting is an important opportunity for team members to express ideas and explain the "how" they have chosen to fulfil the "what" and "why" of their mission. They should be able to freely explore and express new ideas, using their manager as a sounding board. The manager, in turn, has the opportunity to challenge those ideas; make sure the reasoning is sound for what's being done, that there is enough ambition, that the context is taken into account; and verify that the person is not acting out of fear, convention, or habit.

When there's a disagreement between managers and people in their team, I'm sometimes requested to intervene. On one occasion, I was asked to lend my authority in solving a crisis. Sue, who was quite new in the company, and had not yet fully grasped the concepts of subsidiarity, told me that they were doing what they were told to do. I asked her whether she found it logical or useful. Rather defensively, Sue replied that she was not convinced of either. I insisted: "So then, why do you do it?" She became uncertain. That was my opportunity to explain: "Within your responsibility, you have to be convinced of what you're doing. If something seems absurd, question it, explore it, understand it. And if it still seems absurd, do it differently. Never forget why you do something. The "why" is in your mission. "How" you do it can change. It's in your hands." Note how people refine their ideas when they have to defend them.

Best Practice: monthly one-to-one meetings

> *The one-to-one meeting is a good moment for a manager to try to convince their team member of something. Emphasis here on the apt word choice of "convincing", given that the manager has already en-*

trusted his/her team members with specific responsibilities, and thus cannot require things be done in a certain way. There's a fine line between coaching, where the boss will listen, understand and encourage; and management, where the boss will challenge, ask for explanations and express opinions. They can agree to disagree. Bottom line: the final decision is in the hands of the team member.

So in your organisation:

- *Get your managers to meet regularly with their direct reports.*
- *Make sure your managers distinguish between "convincing, challenging and asking for explanation", which they should be doing; versus "requiring a certain action be taken", which they should not be doing.*

Subsidiarity flourishes in an environment of shared common values

For subsidiarity to function well, certain values need to flourish in a company: trust, autonomy and transparency. We're going to briefly consider each of these three.

The value of trust

In my one-to-one meetings, I've noticed how at times there's an evolution of trust. At first some people will stick to what they think I want to hear. They'll only mention the positive things going on and keep me in the dark about other matters out of fear that I might interfere, contradict or lose trust in them. Gradually, people realize that I'm there to help them and that I fully recognize I'm less competent than them as regards their job. As we were instituating subsidiarity in the company, it took almost a year for one of my team members to start hinting at his failures and doubts. Only at that point did the meetings really become useful. We've been having these meetings for many years now, and they're still insightful for me and useful for him. Overall, they're beneficial for the company in helping the patients, our ultimate WHY.

Trust is fundamental and goes both ways. When new employees start in the company, they are trusted by default. No need to earn it. Since we believe they'll be true to their word, we don't need to control or check up on them. We openly share all information and strategies that employees, including new ones need to know.

> ***Best practice: remember that trust towards you can take time***

Ian is so right about trust. First of all he's right in placing importance on trust. It's basic to any human relationship. Secondly, he understands that you cannot "make" people trust you. It will come gradually through actions that manifest you are trustworthy.

So in your organization:

- *Be patient about receiving the trust of your direct reports, knowing this happens over a period of time.*
- *For your part, show trust to others (which is not naivety. See the point on transparency below.)*

The Value of Autonomy

I worked in a company where the expectations for teamwork were over the top. On one occasion, a team wanted to send an important letter. The person in charge not only wanted feedback for his proposal but insisted that we fully agree on every single word. What a painful process, with little added value! After all, consensus isn't about guaranteeing a superlative idea but rather about providing the least painful result for all present.

Autonomy means accepting disagreement and owning a solution as well as the results.

Autonomy is a crucial value for our company. Within their mission, each person is expected to be in the know and make good decisions. Autonomy can be challenging as there's no safety net coming from first having obtained approval.

Decisions are not validated by management but by results. In the business-world, validation is given by the client. If clients see what you do, understand, like, need and can afford it, then they might buy your product. We are validated if healthcare professionals integrate our therapy in their practice and help patients improve their health. That's success in our eyes.

Autonomy requires us to constantly analyse our environment. We glean clues and hints from the environment about risks, challenges and upcoming needs, while the choice of integrating them remains in each person's hands. Maybe there will be team meetings to explore a challenge from various angles and coordinate responses; but everyone fully owns their part of the solution.

Let me note here that autonomy, in a company, is in contradiction to democracy. Having everyone give an opinion on a project within your responsibility and then taking a vote is a recipe for disaster. Those who vote against will be dissatisfied that their opinion is not followed, while the others will fall under the delusion that the thrill of choosing can be disconnected from bearing the burden of the consequences.

Neither is autonomy independence, as that would mean you're alone and can do as you please. Autonomy happens within the context of a purpose, a mission. In autonomy, people work together, with each person bound by their own constraints. Understanding each other's constraints, accepting the other missions is what gives autonomy its meaning.

We can say that autonomy requires an ongoing process, which is why it's a recurring theme in the one-to-one monthly meetings.

Best practice: look to encourage autonomy

Since autonomy necessarily means taking risks, it's important to at least give moral and effective support to those who are growing in autonomy. Ian has wisely identified a specific, regular meeting time to ensure this happens.

So in your organisation:

- *Make sure everyone understands the meaning of autonomy, which is different from democracy and independence.*
- *Be ready to give moral support, especially when starting out with subsidiarity, so that employees will be willing to take on the risk and responsibility of autonomy, while remaining attentive to the roles and needs of others in the organisation.*

The value of transparency

Once trust and autonomy have taken root in a company, then the third fundamental value of transparency is possible, namely, that anybody within the company can know and see what is being done. Transparency reveals projects which are either half-baked or just plain bad ideas. People may shy away from transparency if they've had a micromanager constantly looking over their shoulder, since they're under the impression that the only effective way to get things done is to keep the boss in the dark. Often companies can create a culture of secrecy when managers are too inquisitive or fickle. New employees, therefore, will need to experience how subsidiarity supersedes stealthiness.

There can only be transparency where there is trust. When people are confident they truly have ownership of their mission, then they're not going to feel threatened at the thought of talking about it. They know they get to make the decisions. Even an opinion given by their manager remains just that.

When there's trust and real autonomy, there's nothing to hide. Transparency also builds trust. A manager will have greater trust in a team member who is open about his/her failures, than one who only manifests successes.

We've had employees who love the autonomy and the trust given to them, but hold off from presenting their projects until they're fully completed. This means that for weeks no one knows what they're up to. Their lack of transparency influences their work as they don't seek feedback or permit their ideas to be challenged. The end product is rarely as good as what it could have been. In these cases, a solution needs to be found because subpar work is not acceptable. The direct manager will have to insist again on the advantages and values of transparency and how it is part of our culture.

> ***Best practice: set up a culture of transparency***
>
> *Individual employees are given responsibility, but they are held accountable for their decisions. Transparency gives managers an opportunity to make timely observations and recommendations that might ensure success or avoid costly errors.*
>
> *So in your organisation:*
>
> - *present transparency as a value for your organisation as a whole.*
> - *set the expectation for employees to vet their ideas with their managers in a timely way, while emphasising that the final decision lies with the one with the specific responsibility.*

- *build transparency into the financial system, so that managers have full visibility on the activities and have access to the expenditures of those in their area.*

Values for team leaders

Beside the above-mentioned values that apply to everyone in the company, subsidiarity implies specific values for team leaders, including the CEO. First and foremost, we simply need to be there, ready to listen to and understand our team members. Subsidiarity means that my team can delegate to me some of their responsibilities and I should be able to accept them.

It's fundamental for team leaders to watch against a person taking on responsibilities which are already in someone else's mission. This can be hard to catch, but must be countered as soon as possible. Some people try to be helpful everywhere, which sometimes comes down to power-grabbing. Whatever the motivation, whether it be out of a kind heart or a scheming spirit, it should be nipped in the bud. The manager needs to ensure everyone on the team knows and trusts that their area of responsibility will be defended.

Team leaders also need much patience. What may seem obvious can take time to sink in. Since team leaders cannot impose, they're therefore obliged to explain, challenge ideas, contextualise, explain again and make sure that things become clear. Fortunately, some other things which seemed trivial and useless, and were missed by the manager, will bear fruit without even being noticed.

Building trust is primarily in the hands of the leader. Punctuality is the first sign of trustworthiness. Leaders should also keep their promises. Other valuable characteristics of leaders are straightforwardness, openness, and the capacity to share. Surprisingly enough, one of the most fundamental values is humility. An idea is only as good as its implementation. Leaders need to freely offer ideas, help their team members to grow, encourage and trust, all the while remaining invisible. Team leaders who take the credit are wasting the potential of their teams.

Best practice: build up your team by making them shine

Subsidiarity is about giving people with the competency and actual responsibility the power to make timely decisions. The point of managing a group of people in subsidiarity is empowering them to fulfil their mission to the best of their abilities.

So in your organisation:

- *Inspire your team leaders to grow personally in patience and humility*

- *Help your team leaders to appreciate the value of making others flourish.*

The Common Good as a corollary to subsidiarity

As a political system, subsidiarity developed within a cultural context. There would be a common understanding between people of the same neighbourhood. They would share values and expectations and often had a common religion and history. These commonalities seemed to be necessary for subsidiarity to actually work.

In our company, we encountered certain challenges. If everyone was fully invested and ambitious in their own mission, sometimes they interfered with the mission of others.

For instance, we have a pleasant break room where employees can enjoy a glass of natural orange juice, a cup of coffee, or eat their meal. At one time, people were so occupied with their missions that they were quickly grabbing a bite to eat so as to get back to what they were doing. Dirty dishes piled up, but that wasn't okay. The cleaning lady's mission is to keep our work environment nice so that we can work efficiently. She's not expected to clean up after everyone.

We realised we needed an explicit shared value that could work hand-in-hand with subsidiarity. Historically, one of the other values often found alongside subsidiarity was that of the common good. We spent some time trying to understand if and how it could apply to us. The word "common" applies, since it's a concept which has to be applicable to each and every one of us, whatever our mission, whatever our situation, and whoever we were.

The concept of good was trickier because today this concept 'good' is sometimes understood as linked to circumstances. In the concept of the common good, however, the concept of good seems to transcend specific situations, and remain as a point of reference regardless of the storm or the current crisis. That's how we tried to understand this concept.

We could have spent a long time in our reflections considering that different cultures around the world might have different understandings of the concept of good. As a company, we did not feel the need to go too far down any philosophical rabbit holes, so we decided to align our concept of good with what is generally considered to be good in our Judeo-Christian culture.

We also realised that the common good was not the good of the many against the few or vice versa. On the one hand, one person's good is not to be sacrificed so that many may thrive. On the other hand, neither was the good of one person to be considered more important than the good of many. Our conception is of a balancing act, where the good of all and the good of each person are continually in balance. Easier said than done.

After our reflections, we were ready to spread our understanding of common good throughout the company.

Once the value of common good showed up

Once we began sharing the value of common good as necessary for our organisation, we saw some interesting effects. For instance, when I explain the notion of the common good to new recruits, I like to take the example of our break room. Everyone knows they're expected to clean what they use, as soon as they use it, whether it's a coffee cup or a plate. We are thereby recognising in common that we all benefit from the good of this room. The idea of common good is caring about the others, while caring for one's own responsibility as well.

The common good is not a set of rules, but rather a mentality of taking others into account. There can be some exceptional circumstances when, for instance, someone is entertaining a guest and isn't able to clean up the coffee cups. In that case, they can just leave them dirty where they are. Someone else, usually the next person to come along, will simply pick them up and wash them. Even though they don't know where those cups come from, they trust that the person who left them did so for a good reason, and that by washing them they're helping the common good. This is a trivial example, but it shows in a very practical way how a culture that recognizes the common good is necessary for subsidiarity.

In practice, this means that as people live their mission and carry out their responsibilities, they'll look out for others, to ensure that they're not interfering with their missions. Just thinking about the common good is a way to counter the risk of selfishness that can overcome autonomous people. It's particularly fundamental for people who work together in teams as they carry out their missions.

For instance the marketing team will make sure that the head of production knows what they are doing so that he can organise properly. When a lorry, full of medication, comes to our Belgium plant, those who are available will give a hand to unload it. When someone is off sick, her colleagues will make sure that there are no urgencies unattended. These are but a few examples of how we keep the common good in mind.

The idea of the common good also implies that if someone asks for help, a colleague should consider whether it's possible to chip in. Needless to say, helping to the detriment of one's own mission is to be avoided. Keeping an adequate balance between looking after one's own responsibility, but being aware of other peoples' challenges is a worthy aspect to be thought through and often addressed during the one-to-one meetings.

Challenges to upholding the common good

In practice, the common good turns out to be challenging to maintain since people have different views of what it means to keep a balance between the good of all and the good of each person. People are conscious of what they do for others, such as washing someone else's coffee cup or staying late to help someone out; but they're less aware of the good done by others. Some people started complaining that the common good was always for others and never for them. We realised it was important to underline when it was being put into practice and manifest how each person contributed to the common good.

Upholding the common good is a work in progress, especially in times of stress and crisis, when it's easy to misjudge the concept of good and the impact it can have on others. Our expectation is for each person to do the right thing regardless of their position. Note that the full humanity of each person is called to the task. We're not about simply applying rules or following regulations. We're owning the moment and taking decisions of right and wrong.

Perhaps some people will think we're unfair to ask such a thing of our employees, without giving strict guidelines and a rule to follow. There's the risk of arbitrary decisions since the concept of good can be understood differently at different times, or even manipulated to adjust to each person.

We think we're being fair because we're drawing upon something that is human. Every one of us, in our private lives, is challenged by decisions of right and wrong. What is good for the children? What should I do for my parents? Should I be taking these holidays or should I be going to visit a friend? Should I be buying this type of food or that type of food? Each one of us faces these types of dilemmas. When we invite people to participate in our mission, we're addressing the whole person, including their moral integrity.

Chapter One: Management Tools of Subsidiarity

We can conclude, therefore, that the common good is a necessary cultural backdrop for subsidiarity to be developed in a human and effective way.

Best practice: transmit the value of the common good along with subsidiarity

Subsidiarity and the common good go hand in hand. Employees need to take full responsibility for their mission and yet not lose sight of the group as a whole. Common sense comes in here, as well as the appeal to the analogy of how they make decisions in their family life.

So in your organisation:

- *Make sure your employees know what the common good means in the context of your organisation.*
- *Provide examples of how subsidiarity and common good come together.*
- *Find ways to value and appreciate when the common good is upheld by employees.*
- *Set clear boundaries with your employees to respect the right channels of authority, so as to avoid stepping on the toes of your team leaders.*

> - *Encourage team leaders to watch and protect against people encroaching on the missions and responsibilities of others.*

Resilience

Resilience is a consequence of the two management tools subsidiarity and the common good. We can understand this concept by looking at the natural world, which is adaptable to changing circumstances. Take trees for instance. During the summer, a tree has leaves for its nourishment and growth while, during the winter, it's leafless as a protection against the cold. I'm fascinated at how a tree will twist and bend in the midst of a storm, but keep its integrity and strength. The power to adapt can be found everywhere in the natural world. The human person, throughout the centuries, has also shown incredible resilience, even in extreme conditions such as deserts and the icy poles. We adapt to changing circumstances.

Resilience has been a key choice for our company. We strive to be able to adapt to the unexpected. For us that means having a surplus. Maybe we won't optimise the financial returns, but we'll optimise our survival amidst changing circumstances.

Asking "who will replace you?"

The question: "Who could replace you if you were not able to come in tomorrow?" is a challenging one to even ask. It's possible, though, in a company with subsidiarity.

Every person in the company needs to take care of the possibility that they may not come to work the next day. Each person, in fact, is responsible for thinking about resilience and making themselves replaceable. People may feel out of their comfort zones exploring this avenue, but it's important for resilience, and only possible if trust is truly there.

Sometimes, I'm privy to exciting news before it becomes public. I love it when one of our young women, taking the initiative of my open-door policy, lets me know she's expecting a baby. Maybe she's waiting to tell other people but she wants me to know, slightly afraid of what might happen. I warmly congratulate her and rejoice with her new adventure as a mother.

Given our employees are about 80% women, we often have three or four who are either expecting or away on maternity leave. While reorganisation is certainly implied for the rest of the team, the responsibility and power are in the hands of the mother-to-be. If her mission is indispensable, she needs to determine how it will be carried out during her absence; or if her mission is not too time-sensitive, she needs to spell out the details of putting in on pause.

I'll be developing a facet of resilience in another chapter, when I speak about a responsibility of mine of goading everyone to look for new opportunities.

Best practice: resilience

Resilience is about the capacity to adapt to changing circumstances, something which is often crucial for organisations to move forward. An important aspect of resilience is being replaceable.

So in your organisation:

- *First discern whether enough trust has been built so that employees will not feel too threatened by the request for each person to plan for how they could be replaced.*
- *Then transmit the value of resilience so the context is clear for the request that will follow.*
- *Next, transmit the expectation that employees work out viable replacement plans with their managers in advance of going on leave of absence or sick leave.*

Conclusion

Remember that a mission includes a WHY and a WHAT, but not the HOW and that missions need to align with responsibility.

You've got a recipe for healthy synergy once subsidiarity is successfully linked with the common good and resilience. People will channel their energies towards achieving goods that help both the company and the people within it.

Chapter Two

Leaky Financial Systems vs. Subsidiarity

One of the most important aspects of subsidiarity is aligning responsibility with power, meaning those with missions to accomplish have what is needed to carry them out. Sounds easy? Apparently it's not. Lots of companies go under because of a misalignment here, even though they had once been highly profitable.

In this chapter, I'd first like to trace back with you a number of typically inefficient financial practises I've come across over the years. Then we'll see how working through subsidiarity goes far beyond just plugging up leaks.

Let's start with when I turned 18 and had to make the hard choice of what to study. Biology was appealing for me because it was about real beings that required all their parts to function well. I liked that everything was necessary. Engineering was also attractive because there's no wiggle room for arguing yourself out of a mistake. But I wasn't ready to choose a career, much less a subject that was to endure the rest of my life. So I opted to study business as a way of postponing my choice of industry.

In France, these particular business studies take five years and require the selection of a specialisation. I went for business finance, which makes sure money flows adequately through an organisation to keep it working. Money flow in a company works a little bit like blood in a living being, bringing oxygen and nutrients to every single organ. That implies knowing how the different parts of an organisation work as well as how they operate together as a united whole.

Since I still had no idea of which industry to enter, I reasoned that being in the financial department would give me a view of the entire company, given that every department needs to pay for things.

Business finance has three main purposes.

1. The first purpose is to make sure that the company is profitable and has the cash to operate. This is the object of general accounting and cash management. If you get this piece wrong you go out of business.
2. The second is to cover taxes. The State requires reporting on how much you are making in order to be sure that they can get their (fair?) share. That is the object of fiscal accounting. The State sets the rules which allows it to extract taxes on added value, on your employees' work, on profit, and basically on anything that happens in the company. If you get this wrong, you might have to pay fines and even go to prison.
3. The third purpose is to inform management about what's happening in the company. They need to know the pulse of their business. If you get this wrong, your company won't adapt to the changing

needs, and opportunities and business will dry up. Once again the metaphor of a living organism comes in handy. This last area of finance is called management accounting, or management information system, or even controlling.

The inefficient or "leaky practises" I'm about to mention now have to do with this last purpose of business finance, the controlling part. Top business executives can feel like they need tight controls on things so as to do their job well. I don't think they realise that the very practises they set up actually undermine the efficiency they're trying to obtain.

Leaky Practice Number One: Executives relying on Questionable Data for Major Decisions

Early on in my career, I had an experience which marked the rest of my life. It happened during my first job, which was in the wool industry.

The people in our head office of Paris wanted to know the impact of the thickness of wool on some of their operational parameters. The finance director, the CFO (Chief Finance Officer), therefore asked us to compile wool thickness data over the last few years and present it to upper management. We replied that this was a matter that had never been tracked so there was no relevant information to offer. The finance director came back with: "Management asked for it, so we need to provide it." He proposed that we make up the statistics based on our own estimations. In other words, to tell a lie.

We argued with him that fabricating the information would not be helpful for upper management as they were likely to base their decisions on unsubstantiated, or even misleading information. The CFO insisted that in fact we knew the information that really mattered and were simply illustrating it with numbers.

This interchange led me to draw two important conclusions about finances:

- One, is that numbers are used to tell a story.
- Two, is that management might not get truthful data because of discordant incentives between management and those required to supply the data. In this case, the CFO's career ambitions trumped the supplying of accurate data.

That particular CFO was fired a few months later for being unethical. For my part, when I left that company, I took with me the precious discovery of the risks related to upper management relying upon iffy data.

> *If those in high positions are relying on data supplied by their employees to make important decisions, what guarantees do they have that the data is not only correct but will also remain pertinent?*

Leaky Practice number Two: Budgeting so as to remain relevant and Spending because it's in the Budget

When it comes to investing money and ensuring a healthy cash flow, we have some basic constraints.

- The first is that we have limited resources.
- The second has to do with the fact that there are many people in the company: if one or a few were to grab up all of the resources, that would leave everyone else in a bind.

Let's be very clear here: when I say "resources", I'm talking about money.

Here's a typical scenario when it comes to making budgets. Management wants to optimise the employment of their resources to carry out the strategy they've set. The various departments need to project how much money they'll need and how much profit they'll make with it. Once all of the proposals have been submitted according to some standard format, then the finance department consolidates all the projects, plans and aspirations of the employees. This data goes back up for analysis by general management.

Not surprisingly, the requests for money are usually unrealistically high. That's because each department strives to come across as essential and optimal for the allocation of resources. Moreover, and understandably, everyone simply wants to gain some extra breathing space. Makes me think of horses when they're being saddled: they suck in their breath when the girth is being tightened around their bellies. So you have to wait a few minutes until they exhale or gently knee the horse in the belly in order to be able to tighten the strap sufficiently. It's really not safe for the saddle to come loose once you're already riding, because you could fall off. In the case of adjusting budgets, there will be a to-and-fro with portions being rejected, and others just being modified. In the end, the budget turns out to be a compromise between what people proposed to do and what management determines should be done. It can be hard to gauge whether the "budget saddle" is sufficiently tight for the ride.

During this process, people are all too aware that management could be asking: "If they didn't spend everything the previous year, why would they need something equivalent or greater for the following year?" And it's just that question (spoken or not) that drives people within an organisation to spend every last penny of their budget by the end of the year, whether that's an efficient use of resources or not.

Budgets, therefore, have some side-effects which I find quite terrifying. First, people are judged on their ability to predict the future. If people will be rewarded for their capacity to fulfil their budget, then ambitious budgets will be penalised while overly conservative budgets will be rewarded. However, in reality, business success relies on taking calculated risks adapted to changing circumstances.

Secondly, budgets take time, often months to elaborate. That means a lot of management time and energy are invested in trying to predict the future and negotiating, only to finish with a compromise that pleases no one.

Thirdly, a great idea during budget-making season may very well turn out to be a pretty stupid idea a few months later when it comes time to be implemented. Nevertheless, since there's funding for the proposal in the budget, it may very well go forward anyways.

A local finance director I know told me about how he has to implement a stringent budgetary process that requires specifying when items will be bought and at what price. Not purchasing the items according to these specifications gets labelled as a failure. That often means missing out on simple opportunities. For instance, they had planned to buy tables and chairs for their new offices that were being built. Their provider offered a 50% discount as long as the furniture was purchased a month earlier than planned. Even though the goods could have been delivered when needed, the opportunity had to be foregone as it was outside the budget plans. That was a waste of the company's resources.

> *Isn't it ironic that the way companies make their yearly budgets can be so counterproductive to the efficient running of the business?*

Leaky Practice Number Three: instigating company policies to control employees

Companies are afraid that money, talent or time resources will be wasted in the company. The knee jerk reaction is to come up with more and more rules, or company policies, to make sure that resources are well spent.

For instance, companies often set policies to ensure that people start work on time and don't leave early. This requires enforcement, which involves some employees dedicating time and energy to check up on the others. Furthermore, there may well be penalties for those who arrive late and rewards for those who come on time. (For that matter, rewards and penalties might also be used to encourage budget compliance.) But rewards might turn out to be counterproductive. We need to keep in mind that if a company encourages a certain behaviour, it will discourage another. Taking the case of punctuality, for instance, employees are being rewarded for being in the office on time; however, if employees then spend the next hour having coffee and chatting around, they might be wasting their time with no benefit to the company. If employees only go by what is measured, loopholes are easy to find.. Too often, policies can stifle the creativity and freedom of the employees to adapt to what the company needs to do for the customer.

Rewards and penalties need to be perfectly thought out and adapted to changing times. We're talking about a utopia that will never happen. But in any case, general management experiences a heavy temptation to control its employees through policies.

> *Lots of controls established by management do not guarantee greater efficiency in a company. On the contrary, they might be dooming the company to sluggishly respond to changing demands in the market, something that could seriously affect a company's profitability.*

A Financial management system in line with subsidiarity

Having experienced firsthand the weaknesses of what I've called "leaky practises", I was looking for something which was flexible enough to adapt to reality through time. A system which would: provide the opportunity for meaningful insights to the people who really needed the data; help the company to be profitable and provide access to resources for those who could benefit from them.

Now, I say that is what I wanted, but I was not the chief financial officer or the finance director of the company. Petra has been with the company for over 20 years, having started as an assistant accountant. Throughout the years, she has earned a Masters in Business Finance. She understood the challenges of the company and we shared many of the concerns about the dangers of a financial management system.

Petra also stands out for seeking to understand what is at stake before formulating her own opinion. Even in the most challenging of situations, she'll always start with questions and plug away until she grasps what's going on. She's ready to consider ideas, from the most innovative to the most absurd: a great sparring partner. So we explored together how to set up our management system.

Getting rid of signed purchase orders

(Here we spell out a practice that was already recommended in Chapter One.)

We wanted to have something up and running as soon as possible so that the power-responsibility alignment would be clear to all.

We started by refusing to sign purchase orders.

A purchase order is a document sent to a supplier saying what you want and the agreed price. Before I came on, the previous CEO would sign all purchase orders. I was eager to stop that practice right from my first day as CEO. After all, I had no idea about most of the laboratory materials we were buying. How could I tell if something was a good purchase when I couldn't even pronounce its name? Secondly, by signing off a purchase, I was giving the impression that I was taking on the responsibility. It might be a shared responsibility, but for the person proposing the purchase, it was a diminished responsibility. It sent out the mistaken message that the CEO knows best. Another reason why I'm against signing purchase orders is my limited availability as CEO to sign, meaning hours, days or even weeks might be lost before a purchase of something necessary could be made.

Petra was in agreement that signed purchase orders should be the first thing to go. You're about to see why this did not imply giving a blank check to everyone, closing our eyes, and merely hoping that we would not spend more than we had.

Simple spreadsheets

Our first management system was a simple online spreadsheet: one for each person who needed to make purchases. As long as people didn't go beyond the amounts we had allocated to each of them, they were free to spend what they needed without any additional authorization.

They would organise their allocated amount by project or activities and assign their purchases accordingly. The spreadsheet would allot a code to each purchase order.

As the invoices arrived at the accounting department, they knew that if there was a code it could be paid. Basically, each person in the company could self-authorise their purchases. No more signing.

Just that simple change created quite a revolution. People were used to waiting, negotiating, and explaining. Now they were free to decide and act. In the beginning, some sought out my approval anyway. I would, of course, refuse, explaining that it was their responsibility and not mine. I could offer my opinion if that is what they wanted, but no more than that. They learned to phrase their questions better. Very soon, people realised that they really had the power to decide their purchases.

The spreadsheet made various important things possible: the finance department could ensure that it only allocated existing funds; individual people got to make decisions that matched with their direct responsibilities; and we thereby made evident that we really meant it when we said that we wanted to align responsibility and power.

It was fascinating to observe how people chose to manage their own resources. For instance, Georgina dedicated only a portion of the resources to her activities for the year. As a prudent spender, she tried hard to keep something just in case an unforeseen need were to pop up. There were others like her. We were very happy to discover people who had never really been able to express this thriftiness, a quality so important for managing money.

From then on, we insisted that people manage their business budget in a similar way to their home budget.

We also realised the need to take a special measure to support the Georgina types in the company. For, if at the end of the year, we were to announce that everything they had prudently saved during the year would be wiped out at the start of a new financial year, they would have been quite up-

Chapter Two: Leaky Financial Systems vs. Subsidiarity

set. So thanks to Georgina, and other people like her, we instituted the rule that any savings of one year would be rolled over into the next. That stopped people from trying to use up their entire budget each year. Thriftiness was thereby encouraged and people felt inspired to start saving in one year for the sake of creative projects in a future one.

Thinking more like an engineer, Lucas managed his resources differently. As soon as he was allocated his ceiling for the year, he planned all his activities based upon every last penny allotted to him. That way he could feel all the constraints, and stretch the possibilities to meet his mission. As the months went by, he would reallocate money from one activity to another. By the end of the year, Lucas had not spent everything, but he had certainly maximised his possibilities, something valuable for a company.

Sarah, on the other hand, was a hoarder because her projects would often go over a few years. When she started something, she needed to have the security that she would be able to complete her activities, so she tried to accumulate as much as possible. Sarah viewed every penny spent as her own. And that's a great attitude to have, because it makes her careful about her decisions.

Then there were the more casual spenders. They wouldn't update their spreadsheet until they were reminded by their manager or the accounting department. These types of people were easy to spot, as they weren't taking their financial responsibility as seriously as they could. We realised they would need more time to fully understand the concept of subsidiarity. They appreciated the autonomy and their power to spend, but not necessarily the responsibility which came with it.

Matthew had still another way of handling money. He was a fierce negotiator with our providers. He wanted to do as much as possible with what he had. So every penny negotiated was a penny more for him that he could spend later. There were quite a few people like Matthew who would bargain and negotiate to get the best deal possible. They were proud of their successes and took satisfaction in their capacity to do more.

Some of our suppliers were thereby thrown into confusion. Around Christmas time, they had stuck to sending a bottle of wine or some token of gratitude to the CEO. Suddenly, the CEO was no longer the one deciding and the suppliers realised they should be giving their gifts to someone else in the company.

Some employees did not feel comfortable negotiating, so they sometimes asked one of the negotiators to help them get the best deal for specific contracts or purchases. It was nice to see this dynamic play out.

Alice, the cleaning lady, was remarkable. With her allocated resources, she would decide upon the best toilet paper or the most efficient disinfectant. Her mission is to make sure that employees in the offices have a pleasant place to work in so that they would be efficient. As the kitchen was in her charge, she needed to deal with the problem that one of our two refrigerators was too small for our needs. Alice didn't want to sink all her resources into buying a bigger fridge. So she put the previous fridge up for sale and, with that money, was able to buy the new one, using very little of the money allocated to her. She was creative, thrifty, and completed her mission beautifully. I frequently use her example to illustrate subsidiarity in action.

Given the many different styles of handling finances, we ended up with quite a bit of unspent allocated money at the end of the year. For a company, this can be a problem because allocated money is supposed to be dedicated to seeking opportunities. Underspending can be a sign of missed opportunities. Remember though, from what was said before, that spending everything doesn't guarantee we're spending our resources on the right opportunities.

Looking at the past year, we judged our expenses to be appropriate, and that we simply needed to open up the opportunities to do more. So the following year, Petra and I allocated 10% more money than we had, given that we knew it would not all be spent. This allowed us to give a little more to everyone, so that they could seize more opportunities when they arose. It's a calculated risk that works quite well.

Moving on from spreadsheets

While the spreadsheet budget tool initially worked well for the CFO and others, at a certain point, we realised the need to set up a proper system. Working with the spreadsheet is asking for disaster. It can be messed up or corrupted. We needed to base our system on something more resilient.

Petra and I wanted an off the shelf solution, if possible one that is cloud-based. We looked at accounting packages, integrated management tools, expert systems, and budgeting tools. We wanted a system which would allow each person in the company to manage their own resources. It also needed to be linked with our accounting system, so that each person could see what there was to spend and what was already spent. It was disappointing not to find what we wanted.

And so we looked at the next best option, which we knew ultimately could be a bad one. We looked to develop our own system. Why is that a bad option? Because by building our own system, we need to be sure that the important features are there along with the necessary ones. For example, an important feature is giving flexibility to our employees, while a necessary feature is managing authorised users. This means a major project. Developing an in-house system is also a bad idea because the system maintenance remains in our hands. With an off-the-shelf product, the developers will upgrade the functionality and develop features on their own initiative. If there's a bug, they'll solve it without us even noticing it. Having to develop our own solution was therefore troublesome.

We also didn't really have the time or resources for a big computer project. Fortunately, we knew a young computer scientist full of potential and with real talents, who was willing to do an internship with us for three months. We knew we might be inviting trouble but it was a way to go beyond spreadsheets and maybe achieve a simple cloud solution.

Petra and I thereupon set up an offsite meeting to be able to dedicate a concentrated amount of time to preparing for the computer scientist who would be arriving in a few days. We needed to define what we needed. Something that would permit us to align spending power and responsibility in the simplest way possible. The internship was only for three months and we knew we would have to maintain the product ourselves afterwards.

We wanted the system to be accessible to everyone, so that each person could take their allocated ceiling and dedicate it to planned activities and projects. Each activity would have a unique code to be used for purchases.

We wanted team managers to see all the activities created by the people in their area.

The managers wouldn't need to validate or authorise activities or spending (of course), but could see how things were developing. This is key for transparency, something fundamental to subsidiarity.

We wanted this consolidated view to include the two of us, the CEO and CFO. In a simple glance we would know how much money had been allocated, how it was being spent, and where we were in the current year. We also wanted to be able to see everything on one page.

It was more of a challenge than the intern had bargained for, but thankfully he was up to the task, and, during his time with us, he developed many new skills. In the end we had a resounding success. He understood our philosophy and adapted some areas of what we had proposed, while keeping all the fundamental features needed for subsidiarity. He agreed that he would be available to iron out any bugs and be there to at least maintain the current functionalities as they were.

The intern ended up launching a company to develop a budgeting tool, called Beyond, built around this idea of employee engagement that he had developed for us. As promised, he maintained our product, but as his own solution matured, we were more than happy to switch to his off-the-shelf, cloud-based program, which had all the features we needed and many more.

Best practice: set up a financial system to support subsidiarity

Ian's company started with a simple spreadsheet where each employee having allocated resources could organise their purchases according to activities or projects. This system was accessible to the individual employees as well as the managers.

This method also provides management the opportunity for making calculated risks based on the spending practises of their employees. For instance, Ian just explained why it is a pretty safe bet for his company to allocate 10% more money than they have based on the amount of money that is left over from one year to another. The point is to analyse spending practises so as to be enlightened about possible opportunities in the future.

So in your organisation:

- Get a budgeting tool to ensure:

    a. transparency in the use of financial resources
    b. that employees can live with the help of their budget throughout the year
    c. that management has ongoing up-to-date financial data

- Encourage thriftiness by rolling over the leftover from one year to the next in the case of people not spending everything allocated to them.
- Analyse data from this system to make calculated risks in allocating funds for future years.

Setting up budgets in a subsidiarity framework

Now that we had a fully functional tool, Petra had to devise a way to allocate resources properly, while avoiding the budget pitfalls I've mentioned earlier in the chapter. This is the solution we adopted.

Petra and I get together sometime in October, estimate if sales will be growing or shrinking for the next year, and decide whether we're going to try to keep the same level of profitability. We consider fixed structural expenses, which are under Petra's responsibility. Our savings in the current year along with the estimated savings of the coming year get integrated into this total. The resulting amount is spread out and allocated specifically to each department. It's actually quite simple. Amazingly enough, the whole exercise of preparing the budgets takes no more than half a day.

When the heads of departments receive their allocated portion, they then allocate sums to each person in their area. Once again, there's a different style for each manager. Most often, they allocate sufficiently to everyone and keep back something just in case. Some allocate as much as possible and keep very little for themselves. Others consider that the big decisions are in their hands and therefore allocate smaller amounts to the others.

In my case, I plan to use less than I have. If, during the year, I see one of my managers struggling, I'll have the necessary resources to help. I particularly like having something set aside so that I've got the freedom to respond to some unforeseen opportunity that might arise.

The budget process doesn't end for us in October. A few times during the year, Petra and I revise our estimations. If sales are going better, that means more money can be shared out to the various departments for their use.

Our management team questioned whether it wouldn't be better for them to ask for what they wanted, rather than receiving either more than they had imagined, or less than what they considered they needed.

We responded with the analogy of a salary. When someone works, he gets a salary. Perhaps it doesn't turn out to be enough for what he would like to do, or it might very well allow the possibility of setting aside money for some great project. In either case, it's the salary itself that allows a person to calibrate what he does. This matched our idea of giving money directly to departments and people. They have a mission, and an available amount to make that mission happen. The allocated amount empowers them to fulfill their mission, which is their responsibility. Of course, Petra and I might sometimes be off with our calculations, but there's wiggle room for some marginal negotiations in those cases. With some years of experience behind us, I can now confirm that our way of allocating resources is a quick and satisfactory way to prepare budgets.

We also have a B plan should we hit a crisis or a stronger dip in sales than anticipated. We need a quick and efficient way to make the right decisions to reduce spending. For that, we rely on our employees who know best where savings could be made.

I had worked before in a company that went through turbulent times. The CEO responded by suspending all travel.

The travelling budget was quite large, so by stopping that line of expense, he hoped to weather the storm. Unfortunately, he chose poorly. Even though some travel was not essential, some trips were indeed necessary to ensure sales, so the company took a severe dip in sales. Taking a centralised decision seemed easy, but it turned out to be bad for the company.

In subsidiarity, we're convinced that in the case of saving money, the ones closest to the activity will know what to do. They could cancel one of their activities or negotiate with a provider. If they understand the challenge, then they'll know how to step up to it.

Best practice: allocate funds in line with subsidiarity

You need to analyse the possibilities, make calculations regarding the future year and then keep abreast of the situation throughout the year. Part of the effort involves relying on your employees to seize opportunities or determine specific cutbacks should the finances require it.

So in your organisation:

- *Stop "budget seasons" by allocating funds instead.*
- *Review your financial situation during the year to assess if adjustments are necessary.*

- *Inform your employees when additional funds are available or cutbacks have to be made but leave the specifics for them to work out.*

Conclusion

Over many years of personal experience, I witnessed again and again the flaws of standard management systems. All too often, good resources get leaked unnecessarily to the detriment of the company. There's a lack of resilience instead of growth and the capacity to adapt to fluctuations in the market. By the time I became CEO, I was convinced there was a more productive way to guide the company, and I found it in subsidiarity.

When the missions of your employees align with the matching power for them to make the necessary decisions, then a wealth of creativity, positive energy and loyalty is unleashed throughout your entire business. It's a win-win situation: on the one hand, the employees are freer, more engaged, more productive and happier in their work and, on the other hand, the business as a whole prospers.

Chapter Three

The CEO in Subsidiarity

Now that I've passed the age of 50, I'm struck by how often my friends ask about where the time has gone, while I still have the feeling that time goes by slowly. Part of my job is to try to get bored.

Yes, bored.

I've already explained how an organisation based upon subsidiarity spreads out the responsibility, leaving very little weight directly upon my shoulders. As CEO I ask what may seem to be a curious question about any work I consider taking on: "If this is important for our business why am I doing it?" A few prior questions make sense of my approach: "Shouldn't the organisation be able to look after this?" If the answer is yes, then I ought to find a way for somebody competent, enthusiastic, and willing to pick up this necessary challenge. Otherwise, if what I'm doing is not that necessary, then why on earth am I doing it?

Furthermore, if what I'm doing needs to bear fruit, that will often imply work to be done over time. If I answer yes to any of these questions, then I need to give this challenge to someone else in the company.

When I become too busy, that's a signal to me that something's the matter. A typical pathology of CEOs is being hyper-busy while everyone else is twiddling their thumbs. I've worked in a company like that. The CEO with his close management team had their time full. They ran from one task to the next, signing authorisations, talking about strategy, worrying about the past, the present and the future; meanwhile, the rest of the underworked and "pretending to look busy" employees were wondering what to do. I would wait hours on end just to be able to talk with the CEO about some pressing issue which needed his input and authorisation. In fact, my days were spent waiting.

I get to be free only once everybody else is occupied. My first task is to make sure that everything is being done and that everyone else is part of the solution. That's why an onset of boredom is a sign for me that something is going right. Having time available lets me do things.

Now I'm ready to explain what I do.

> **Best practice: accept that having spare time goes with your job!**
>
> *There's an important underlying attitude in Ian's description. He has both the presence of mind and courage to give himself permission to have spare time while seeking to make sure others are occupied. Undoubtedly he knows his view goes against a current mindset of what makes for success, yet his reasons are sound.*

So in your organisation:

- *Take time to consider whether you are convinced by Ian's viewpoint and if so make the decision to act similarly.*
- *If you decide to have a similar approach then assess your workload in light of the responsibilities proper to your role using Ian's questions to determine which ones you should be keeping:*

    1. *Would you need to do it long term?*
    2. *While you're doing it, would you be unavailable for the rest of the company?*
    3. *Would this eat a big chunk of your time?*

If you answer yes to any of these questions, then discern how someone else could accept this responsibility within their mission. (Note: I originally had used the word "delegate" in this sentence, but then Ian explained to me that delegating doesn't match with their concept of mission. Rather, people accept new responsibilities in their missions. In that way they have the necessary authority and power to properly fulfil what is asked of them.)

What falls to me as CEO

For one, the fundamental management tools fall under my domain. It's up to the CEO's choice whether the company is an autocratic centralised effective power machine or a flexible, intelligent, creative and efficient machine. Or somewhere in between.

As you know, subsidiarity and the common good were two of my choices. I'm responsible for upholding them and making sure they are fully functional.

I also need to keep the values and management principles alive. My mission is to make sure I have the right organisation in place so that the company's mission can be fulfilled; but just like the team leaders within the company, I need to make sure that all of my responsibilities are properly distributed. Everything that needs to be done must be covered by someone within my team, and thus the organisation of my team is fundamentally my mission. This is an ongoing process: tweaks or changes could occur anytime; or changing circumstances might require more profound modifications.

The organisation chart is an important tool for us. It allows us to capture who does what and how the teams are organised today. As you will see it reflects our organisation in subsidiarity where those who have the most responsibility and power are those who are most closely tied with the actual challenges.

Team leaders are there to give support as necessary, and can be relied upon if team members need to delegate to their manager some situation that cannot be managed within their realm of responsibilities and power. I, along with my team members, need to understand the challenges of each member of the team with which we have been entrusted, so that we can truly be of service to them.

Our organisation chart is in the shape of a tree. Each team member is like a leaf, while each team leader is like a twig, giving support to those leaves. The managers who have team leaders are like branches giving support to their team. I'm at the very bottom of the organisation chart, like the trunk of a tree, there to give support to all the branches.

When we present this organisation chart to new employees we explain that in a tree, those who truly do the work, are the leaves. They take in the energy of the sun and use it to extract CO_2 from the atmosphere, get rid of the oxygen, and use the building blocks of carbon to make everything necessary for the tree. To do their work, the leaves need to be spread out to maximise their exposure to the light, and twigs and branches are there to give them the most reach and the most support possible. The branches will help to spread the work of the leaves throughout the tree and will count on the support of the trunk. This image of a tree reminds us of our company's values and organisation, hopefully, appreciated by all.

I like to keep the organisation chart up-to-date. I make sure to get a photo from new employees, and update the chart. Doing this allows me to know who is in our company, who is participating in the challenge of our mission.

Another of my responsibilities is to make sure that everyone in the company has the opportunity for growth. Having the same responsibility and the same mission for too long can be stagnating. After a few years of experience, people have a different outlook, and much more talent. Some are eager to take on new challenges. In a small company, this can be difficult, as there are just so many ways to reorganise a team. I try to make sure that we're creating new work opportunities for existing employees, because we want to keep the best talent within the company and allow the company to grow, taking into account the unique experiences of each person.

I'm careful to keep all our employees employable, so, if someone wishes to leave the company, they'll be a good fit for attractive opportunities. If we develop employees with too specific skills and idiosyncratic ways of doing things, they'll remain in the company not because they choose to stay, not because they appreciate the challenge, but because it's the only job they know how to do. Some of our employees have been with us for over 20 years. In my opinion, they shouldn't still be here merely because they've nowhere else to go. They should be staying by choice, with a willingness to fight for their mission.

We encourage people to grow their talent stack. That means their unique blend of talents which make them distinct from everyone else. For instance, we give access to any type of training someone sees as necessary, like language lessons, during office hours for anybody in the company who wishes to take them. The employees don't always need those languages for their current position, but we know that this could give them opportunities for tomorrow. Perhaps these will be beneficial for our company, with our employees gaining in confidence, thinking differently and exploring new horizons or maybe they will just be a personal boost. I'm not interested in having prisoners work for our organisation, but rather capable and willing partners who stay with us because here is where they can best express their talents, unique personality and experience, and grow as human beings in the process.

> **Best practice: spread a personal growth mindset throughout your organisation**
>
> Ian appreciates the value of employees who freely choose to work for his organisation. So he encourages them to grow their personal talents and gifts and thus "stay employable". Note also the personal interest he takes in his new employees in learning their names. No doubt all of this helps in creating a welcoming work environment, where they experience they are treated with the respect due to persons.
>
> So in your organisation:

- *design and explain an org chart with yourself at the bottom, including everyone's name and photo.*
- *learn the names of your employees.*
- *encourage people to grow their talent stack.*
- *strive to create new work opportunities for current employees.*

Making sure things happen

I'm responsible for all of these aspects of the organisation, but they don't take up much of my time. Even updating the organisation chart is fun and quick. So what else do I do?

In our group, we have many different ways of doing things. Some people like to talk and ponder, plan and scheme, but sometimes struggle to implement. Others will jump into action, and lack the planning. My ongoing challenge is to make sure that things happen. Ideas may abound, but the valuable ones are those which become reality. I'm very interested in bringing new ideas from the incipient phase to actual implementation. Finding the right person within the company, or deciding to create a new position is an important step to make things happen. Trying to make an idea happen by myself, by doing it, is a sure route to failure. Not only am I incompetent in many cases, but if I dedicate too much time to a single idea I won't be available for my overall mission.

When an idea comes up, even within a team, I've got to make sure we're not talking idly. Doing, and doing it well is crucial.

From time to time, I need to shake the status quo, challenge ways of doing things.

Technology is an interesting way to keep people alert. If we always do things the same way, we'll stop thinking about them and opportunities for improvement will be lost.

For instance, I strongly suggest the usage of cloud tools. In-house servers are a point of fragility for companies. Though these tools fall within the responsibility of each person, I provide a direction to the technological culture in our company.

I challenged my team to stop using Microsoft Word, and to use a fully cloud-based word processor instead. Most people were reluctant as Word is a basic reference point in the business world. Nevertheless, our person in charge of quality procedures rose to the challenge. They had hundreds of procedures regularly updated from the word format. He took on an intern for a couple of months to modify all the Word documents into the new cloud format. A few months later, as the coronavirus hit the world, he didn't hide his pleasure at having a fully cloud-based document system. Our employees were able to work out of their homes, as they had access to all of the documents they needed.

We also use a mix of communication tools. Emails, direct messages, video calls and the like. I had been looking at Slack, a communication tool. I didn't really understand it, but had the intuition that it could be helpful. One Thursday, I sent an email to everyone in the company, informing them that, from the following week, we would no longer use email or Skype for internal communication. Some people panicked, others were amused, and some observed ironically that this way of imposing a new tool was at odds with subsidiarity. They had a point.

Nevertheless, I decided to impose it, as my responsibility is to make sure that we don't grow old with our tools. Sometimes, a friendly push is necessary. Over the following months, people discovered the power of this new tool and adapted it to their needs within their responsibility and power. Today they wouldn't go back. And once again, in the midst of the coronavirus, having this fully implemented meant we were fully equipped for working from home. This gave resilience to our company.

> **Best practice: apply a growth mindset to the organisation as a whole!**
>
> *It's amusing to consider how Ian's somewhat discombobulating innovations are in line with subsidiarity! His two examples of the fully cloud-based server and the communication tool Slack provided improvements for the entire organisation, which falls within his sphere of responsibility.*

Chapter Three: The CEO in Subsidiarity

So in your organisation:

- *Be on the lookout to make things happen!*
- *Encourage an environment where new ideas are both welcomed and brought to completion.*
- *For your part, consider well what tools would serve to improve your organisation as a whole and then implement them. Improved technology is a good place to start.*
- *Shake up the status quo to instigate growth and improvement.*

Redesigning the office space

The way we work is another of my responsibilities. Three years ago, we needed new offices because we were expanding. I thought that having an open space would help us to experience better our values of transparency and trust. Many people were reluctant to switch from a closed office to an open space, but that was my call.

When we finally moved, we made sure that each team could organise their tables within the open space, so as to adapt to their own challenges. The open space would represent a blank sheet of paper where each team could express its needs. This allows teams to change the way they come together, and interact.

Over these last three years, tables have moved, departments have spread, with the open space being the canvas on which we draw our organisation. This constraint has now been fully integrated. During the coronavirus lockdown, with people required to work out of their homes, many employees regretted the loss of the social interaction we are now accustomed to having at work.

As you can see, an aspect of my job is to be a disruptor and to propose constraints which allow creativity to grow.

Another responsibility entails trying to keep the pulse of the company. Are we doing what we could be doing? Are we being efficient and intelligently looking at the opportunities or challenges? Are people getting overstressed? Are there any unhealthy politics happening within the company? Do people really feel safe and free within their mission? Just being there, talking about the weather or current affairs, helps me to pick up vibes.

At the end of the day, all these responsibilities don't amount to much activity, which is fine. I invest a big chunk of my time to be available for my team.

In our organisation, decisions are taken without me. Things happen and risks are taken without my participation. Sometimes I wonder whether I could go on holiday for months on end, and the company would continue working. However, ever since we started working by subsidiarity, people have experienced the need for feedback, especially as they can go on for weeks before seeing any results. They need to know if what they're doing is coherent with our overall mission. They need to trust that there is a captain in the boat, and that's my job.

Best practice: keeping your ear to the ground within the company

In this section Ian has shared with us just how attentive he is to what is going on in his company. Maybe you won't feel the need to redesign the office space as Ian did, but the point is to be watchful for opportunities, being open to new ways of doing things. Through his list of questions we can pick up the value of his physical presence among his employees. He catches a lot, first because he is there amidst his employees, and second because he makes it a point to be observant of what is going on around him. Ian is able to do this because he hasn't packed his schedule with responsibilities that suck his time, attention and energy.

So in your organisation:

- *Keep an eye out for what is going on. Ian's questions can be helpful to know better what you're watching for:*

    - *Are we doing what we could be doing?*
    - *Are we being efficient and intelligently looking at the opportunities or challenges?*
    - *Are people getting overstressed?*

- *Are there any unhealthy politics happening within the company?*
  - *Do people really feel safe and free within their mission?*

- *Regularly "take your own temperature":*

  - *Do you have the interior peace and space to be capable of noticing what's going on around you?*
  - *Is your to-do list so demanding that it sucks the bulk of your energy and attention? If yes, what can you take off this list to free you up?*

- *It might be helpful to dedicate specific moments in the day to consider what you have observed and whether there is something to do about it.*

Dedicating time to meet with team members

Every four to six weeks, I'll have a one-to-one meeting with each one of my team members. Whether it lasts one to eight hours, I'm there for my people. We'll explore their current challenges, the situation of their mission, the constraints of their team, and whatever they wish to talk about.

This is how I discover what's being done, thought processes behind decisions; arising challenges; and employees' current understanding of their mission.

Each person within my team approaches this meeting differently. Some focus on what they do, others on their challenges, still others on their teams. Meanwhile, I'm a tree trunk providing support. I'm a sounding board for new ideas, doubts, and ambition. I also need to challenge, coax and encourage.

At the end of our meetings, each person should feel encouraged to continue their mission, knowing they have my backing as CEO, that their actions participate in our overall mission, and that they can truly express all their talents.

Some examples of one-to-one meetings

I've picked the following examples as a way of illustrating the variety, richness and breadth of our one-to-one meetings, and how they are adapted to the personality, set of skills, expertise, and especially the mission of each person.

My longest meeting will always be with Fiona, who became the head of market development, who has one of the biggest groups within the company. She has organised her group into different teams along country and project lines. These teams have different sets of challenges related to diverse countries.

During our meetings, Fiona fills me in about what is being done, and then we explore together the options which have been taken. We're in an industry where the other players are huge multinationals who mold the health narrative. Fiona therefore has the challenge of being the underdog and managing a powerful multicultural team. She thinks a lot. She continuously challenges her team members as to why they are making certain decisions. She needs to plan well so as to ensure that things are done intelligently. Like the rest of us, she works with the advantages and the challenges of subsidiarity.

Fiona will share her thoughts with me about her team leaders. While recognising their challenges, she's trying to help them grasp the big picture and trust in themselves. We'll often have long discussions on subsidiarity, especially when Fiona thinks that things should be done differently. Fiona often needs to try to convince her people to be less ambitious, but more thorough in what they are planning to do. She helps them think ideas through, understand and increase the efficiency of what is being done.

The meetings are shaped differently for Petra, our head of finance. Initially she was reluctant even to have these formal one-to-one meetings, given that she frequently seeks immediate feedback from me. Nevertheless, as time passed, she asked to have at least one such meeting every few months. I was delighted, given that I don't want to impose unwanted meetings on anyone. At this point, we have regular one-to-one meetings.

Petra goes over all the current affairs just to ensure that I know what is happening. She likes us to explore solutions to

Chapter Three: The CEO in Subsidiarity

more tricky situations. Petra realises that each team member has specific strengths, weaknesses, blindspots, and specific expectations. Having the right person in the right place is an ongoing challenge, especially in a complex multi-national environment that makes administrative matters more burdensome.

No surprise that my meetings with Lucas, our head of production, are extremely structured and efficient since he has an engineer's mindset. They typically last just over an hour. Before each meeting, he'll send me a full report, including the latest metrics update. From one meeting to the next, he'll tweak his data and his dashboard. Lucas even has metrics on subsidiarity.

Production is less my area of expertise, so I stick to challenging him in regards to matters of management and logic. Though Lucas was already applying subsidiarity before it was implemented company-wide, he now experiences the freedom to share responsibilities that he had thought he had to keep for himself, and to meet with each member of his production team about their particular mission. Lucas makes the most of our meetings to understand what is happening within the company, in order to gain insight about production needs.

Once Lucas started his meeting by stating "I have failed my mission". It was true, we had suffered from a couple of products being out of stock. He therefore explained that he had explored why it had happened and what he was putting into place to avoid it happening again. I also showed him that sometimes he would bend backwards to help some colleagues and did it to the detriment of his own mission. In this instance he had waited patiently for another department when he should have been more forceful.

Often, when I spot shortcomings, or I hear that one of my managers is doing something wrong, I will generally wait till our next one-to-one meeting to bring it up. For instance, one of my managers was putting too much pressure on her team. When I sat down with her I started by asking her about her team and realised she was unaware of the situation. I therefore told her that something might be happening and encouraged her to take it into account. From then on it was an ongoing challenge to help her become aware of how her style was affecting her team. Being able to give negative feedback in a constructive way is an important part of being a manager.

During our meetings we also often explore the challenges some of their team members might have. I always listen very carefully to how the manager talks about a person. There is a fine line between criticising and seeing the weaknesses. In the former, there is a sense of superiority and minimising the person's abilities, in the latter it is trying to objectively assess how to find a way for a person to express their full potential whatever it may be.

The specific rhythm of the one-to-one meetings depends on each person. For instance, for a while, I met with Peter almost weekly, back when he was the head of our research and development team on the development of proteins. In our efforts to expand the business, we had worked out with him that he would explore areas of diversification in the biotechnology world, since he knew it so well. We had also offered Peter the chance to obtain an MBA degree. While Peter was studying and looking into the possibilities, we would meet on a normal six-week basis, but as Peter was finalising his MBA, he honed in on a specific start-up idea of diagnosis with DNA. Given the need to get in start-up mode, our one-to-one meetings increased in frequency to every one or two weeks. Peter needed quick feedback, given the urgent matters that were springing up.

Best practice: dedicate the time needed for one-on-one meetings with your team members

There's a lot packed into Ian's description of what is entailed in these meetings. Ian has freed up his time so that he can be fully available for as long as needed in these regular appointments. This is where he has an opportunity to influence his direct reports in an adequate way. We can imagine Ian's team members experience someone they can count on to challenge and encourage them in their work, while always leaving them the breathing space to take their own decisions.

So in your organisation:

- Get the message across that you will be available in these regular one-on-one meetings for as long as your team members need.
- Let each of your team members decide the agenda for these meetings and accept what they come up with.
- Remember to be patient during a first period of building trust. Over time, your team members will likely bring more points to the table and more significant ones at that.

Understanding the world and being on the lookout

My one-to-one meetings take about 25% of my time. So I'm still available for other matters.

An important aspect of my job is to be on the lookout. Our world is ever-changing, expectations of patients and healthcare professionals are in flux, science is seen as the new yardstick of truth and falsehood, and even fake news affects many people. Evidently, the new coronavirus episode is fundamentally changing the world of health.

On a yearly basis I try to reflect about subjects which I can explore and implement. One of them is how to work with subsidiarity. Another one was seeing how the common good could help the company. For two years I've been working on trying to understand how perceptions about health and medicine can be changed, given that we are a challenger.

Last year, my yearly project was to share my experience on subsidiarity, hence this book.

I strive to understand trends and situations. One way is to participate in events outside of our normal day-to-day work. I'll deliberately put myself into new or different situations where I don't understand what's going on. For instance, I participated in various conferences, workshops and organisations, such as a blockchain conference, just to pick up new ideas; an Italian fringe medical workshop; and the normative work on biomimetics for a few years. This forces me to stretch my reasoning and understand another aspect of how the world works.

Keeping the big picture

I investigate whether there are opportunities beyond our typical environment. I follow the news and try to understand what is happening. Unfortunately, the news is all too often a predigested and misleading view of the world.

Other ways of learning about what's going on in the world and discovering new opportunities are blogs, podcasts, videos etc. The people on my list of podcasters challenge me and help me understand the ever-changing world we live in.

I try to have a network of people in order to hear their ideas and discover new perspectives. These friends with different viewpoints in numerous countries and various industries, are accessible through a simple call or some sort of social media. They allow for a rich exchange of ideas and keep me from falling into a simple, one dimensional understanding of the world. The wide contrast allows for capturing opportunities and trends.

I share these thoughts, discoveries and questions with my management team. I count on their feedback while also challenging them to keep on the lookout for opportunities. For instance, when I travel and visit a production plant, I'll come back and share my thoughts and experiences with our production manager. He's not expected to implement anything specific, but this input helps him to continue thinking and refine the methods he uses to fulfil his mission.

Taking into account narrative bubbles

One of the greatest challenges to understanding the world is our own personal narrative bubble, which is our means of understanding the world. It allows each of us to realize where we come from through our personal history, and recognize what changes occurred to bring us to our current situation. Unconsciously we create filters to understand current affairs and be enlightened about the possibilities laying before us. Some can be exciting and motivating, but others can look dangerous and menacing.

These narratives are pervasive throughout society. Whatever the newspaper, magazine, or media, none of them just give facts. The facts are set within a context that illustrates their own narrative.

If the media is left-leaning, there's a vision of an oppressed world where victims are being exploited. We'll learn about victims and how they're mistreated.

If the media is right-leaning, there's an attitude of obtaining success through one's own efforts. In that case, we'll be told stories about self-made people and other aspects of the economy or politics which illustrate their worldview.

In both cases matters like fashion, sport or food will mainly be addressed if they can illustrate in some way their worldview.

Even in this book, I'm choosing examples according to the narrative that convinces me. I'm trying to explain the advantages of subsidiarity, the common good, resilience and the importance of a flexible and multifaceted strategy.

Perceiving that the world as overlapping narrative bubbles is itself a narrative bubble. I could explain the history of ideas, how the recent technological changes and the speed of dissemination of ideas has brought us to this present state, where everyone has a platform to defend their worldview. Even though we're receiving an open and rich wellspring of ideas, we no longer have access to simple facts anymore, and we're thereby susceptible to being swept over by the next dominant ideology.

A few years ago, I took part in a peaceful gathering of a couple hundred thousand youth. It was nice and friendly with people from all around the world, mainly boy scout types.

A news crew approached us and explained they'd been sent out by their editor specifically to find examples of violence and fighting. They'd been looking for hours to no avail. So they asked us if we knew of any place where something wrong was happening. They had a story, they had a narrative to illustrate, and they were desperately trying to find facts which could fit their view.

Narrative bubbles are not a misrepresentation of the world, but rather the reality in which each of us lives. Understanding this context allows us to find opportunities within the narrative, as well as the opportunities beyond. I'm conscious of narrative bubbles while reading through the news, thus I try to separate the facts from the story being told. Often I'll investigate whether what is being reported is a real trend or something which is deliberately being fomented.

I dedicate much of my free time in an effort to understand the world and how each one of us understands it. My interest is in trends where my company could be of service. For instance, there are new narratives developing about patient choice. Should patients participate in the type of health they have? They choose to be vegan. In a similar vein, could they choose what medicine they want?

Best practice: keeping your ear to the ground outside of the company

Not only does Ian closely observe what is going on within his organisation, he is also watchful of what's happening in the world. New insights and opportunities arise for his company thanks to this practice. Note his work is twofold: first he dedicates time and attention to catch trends then secondly he does the exercise of considering how these could be opportunities for his company. And he's not working alone. Ian speaks about his observations and ideas with his team members.

So in your organisation:

- *Reflect about whether you are employing sufficient means for staying informed about what's going on "out there". You will want to enrich the input by using diverse sources and viewpoints.*
- *Identify your own narrative bubble and try to reach beyond it.*
- *Apply your critical thinking skills to detect the narratives of the news sources and do your homework to get to the bottom of apparent trends. Are they real or are they being created?*

- *Dedicate time to considering how you can best glean ideas and opportunities for your work in light of the world's happenings.*
- *Share your observations and ideas with your team members.*

The Go Game

When I was younger, I enjoyed playing games. They're a way to put skills, thought and reflection, into practice and see results on a short timescale. I played many hours of the video game "Age of Empires". The player starts with a simple civilization and few resources and has to grow the civilization to dominate the world. In an hour or two, a strategy can be deployed, and the player implements a tactic to gather the right mix of resources and the correct balance of people in their civilization. Even though this was a very crude representation of life, it allowed me to explore different options, and have real-time feedback.

The ancient Chinese Go Game structured my worldview. Winning is not about attacking the opponent, but covering more of the board than the other. The playing board has 361 intersections, representing the infinity of the world. The game consists in placing black stones or white stones, with one colour assigned to each player. No stones are stronger than any other. Taking turns, each player places a stone on one of the intersections. The stones can be laid anywhere on the board where there's a free intersection, but once they are laid they cannot be moved. The importance of individual stones depends upon the ones nearby. Many stones together can form a chain to limit a territory claimed by the player.

As the game unfolds, certain stones take on more value, while others are abandoned. At the beginning of the game, it's impossible to predict how the game will turn out, but good players will spot patterns and invest more stones where the potential of gain is likelier, as well as abandon stones that no longer serve. Stones also need to be placed that will create opportunities later on in the game.

I use the Go Game model in developing strategies and creating opportunities. When an idea needs to spread, or an opportunity has the potential to develop, it requires supporting stones. Even before the opportunity or idea exists, just being there can be a way to foster an opportunity.

Some CEOs will have a more confrontational model of the world, like the game of chess. Markets need to be conquered and competitors need to be vanquished. The Go game, on the other hand, recognises that diversity exists and that coexistence is the reality of life.

What I like about the Go Game is the infinite possibilities. In trying to make the world a better place, a fully defined strategy will not work. The present is full of changing parameters which create havoc in the best-defined plans. The idea of infinity illustrates uncertainty. The world has events and people constantly making an impact and changing up the game. So it's paramount to keep adapting, and maintain multiple fronts open.

The future is always uncertain, so the expression "the fog of war" matches most initiatives while they're in the making. As the future becomes the present, and uncertain occurrences become probable events, we discover a landscape of new opportunities and new situations.

Driving the strategy of diversification (a significant aspect of resilience)

The world is a changing place. Today's opportunities might not bring the desired results; whereas the doubts of yesterday might lead to the next success. Good strategy means keeping many fronts open at once, like the stones on the Go board. Our company tries to keep many initiatives happening in parallel. Each one brings the potential of establishing new territory, with everyone cooperating in the expansion.

The strategy of diversification matches with the expression of not putting all our eggs in the same basket. The idea is for initiatives to be spread out and ready to grow, while also being easy to abandon, so that those involved can quickly move on to something else. It's the diversification of opportunities. As CEO, I ask employees to keep their options open and try, try again.

Our organisation in subsidiarity is particularly suitable for the strategy we follow. People are free to implement the local strategies they see fit. The transparency and flow of data

Chapter Three: The CEO in Subsidiarity

within the organisation allows each one to adapt their activities and initiatives. The decentralised decision-making permits adaptations to the reality on the ground. The right to fail allows for the placement of a stone towards some tentative opportunities, and moving on if they don't bear fruit.

A pitfall for some CEOs is to have a pet strategy where they invest all their efforts and become blind to other opportunities. What happens if they choose the wrong strategy?

A company within our industry was experiencing reduced sales. They hired some of the best consultants to analyse the situation and came to the conclusion that they were being affected by fake news. When their investment in an online presence to reverse the trend proved unsuccessful, the CEO was replaced as no other plan was in place.

We clearly recognise that we don't know what will work. We believe in our initiatives and we'll put sufficient energy behind them, but we're aware that many initiatives will not be as groundbreaking as we wish they could be.

A case in point has to do with our need for medical doctors to understand our therapy. We therefore strive to teach it in as many ways as possible: online and offline, with seminars, with groups of doctors sharing their ideas, through publications, in hospitals, with private clinics and so on.

An initiative which worked remarkably well was sharing our therapy in private clinics. The opportunity arose when a doctor contacted us from one of these clinics. As we trained her, we met quite a few of her colleagues who were also eager to learn. We thereby discovered that these clinics needed original, cutting edge therapies to propose to their patients. The doctors were more than pleased to be able to integrate our therapy within their proposed strategies.

We go down many paths, have a number of small successes and from time to time are lucky enough to encounter a significant new avenue. When a promising opportunity arises, employees are able to add resources and re-allocate their time and effort to make it flourish.

As CEO, my job is to grasp the potential of our opportunities and support initiatives, by defending each person's area of responsibility and maintaining subsidiarity.

Through the culture of the company, I encourage people to avoid unique solutions. Instead, they're stimulated to explore, make attempts, fail, try something else and then continue and develop what does work.

> **Best practice: Determine your key strategy such as diversification and communicate it adequately**
>
> *Ian has spelled out how to not put all your eggs in a basket. Already, a company in subsidiarity provides for diversification because there are so many minds free to come up with ideas and respond to rising challenges. Furthermore he has created a work environment where there is an expectation for employees to diversify. Sounds like a happening place!*
>
> *So in your organisation:*

- *Reflect about whether you have any pet strategies that hold you and your organisation back.*
- *Transmit the expectation to your employees as regards your key strategy. For example, if it's diversification, communicate that they should:*

  - *seek for multiple solutions,*
  - *be creative,*
  - *adjust to changing circumstances and cease opportunities,*
  - *take calculated risks.*

Helping to recruit the right people

We're looking for people, not diplomas. In my mind, recruitment is one of the most challenging tasks in the business world. The implications resulting from whom we hire make such a big impact on what we can do as a company.

I don't participate in every interview nor do I meet in advance every person who'll be joining the company. Recruiting is not my responsibility, nor is it the responsibility of human resources. We've intentionally made each team leader responsible for recruitment to their team, as well as the professional development of the people on their team. They're supposed to ensure people hired by our company succeed in expressing their full potential as a person.

Some people will ask for my input when they're recruiting and I'm happy to oblige. They know the final decision is theirs, even if I were to end up having strong reservations about a candidate.

The following is a scenario of my typical involvement in the hiring process.

4 pm. The candidate arrived and was welcomed a few minutes ago. She's now in a meeting room waiting to be interviewed for the third time. She's a bright young doctor who just finished her PhD. Mary has been shortlisted as a candidate for our communication department. Today, I'll try to form an opinion about her human values.

During an interview I'll likely ask: "Why do you want to work for us?"

I hope to hear that they've researched the company, appreciate our values, are excited by our mission, want to make the world a better place, and believe that they have the unique set of skills to match our needs. Too often, I get the answer that they want to work for us because they are motivated. Motivation can be fickle. In some companies, it can be stifled within a week. We know that motivation is important, so we will always try to keep it alive, but that demands a continuous effort on the part of the company.

I don't concern myself with the person's technical expertise for the mission. If a candidate has come this far in the interview process, then I assume they have the competence and potential for what we need. I'm trying to evaluate whether the candidate has the potential for listening, understanding, and adapting to a situation. I'll also try to discern whether we share values like the common good and if the person will be able to adapt to our subsidiarity model.

My first question is "Who are you Mary?" Mary hesitates. She realises she's not being asked something typical like what she's done before or where she's from. It's a more fundamental question. She asks "What do you mean? Do you want to know about my studies or what I've done?"

She does well to start with a question, trying to clarify what has been asked. She's not jumping impulsively down the first road she sees open.

In this interview, I'll be exploring her capacity to understand, to react under stress, her openness to others and whether she could fit into our values and management system.

Causing stress isn't much of a challenge for me. As CEO, I'm mistakenly perceived as the person with a right of life or death over someone's potential employment (even though I'm only a consultant in this process). I also don't make much of an effort to be friendly during recruitment meetings.

I'll ask many questions that only require brief responses, but might possibly let the answers go on for a while. In one instance, someone spoke for nearly half an hour with just my first question. It was a speech that didn't reflect well on that person because there was no sign given of needing to listen and understand.

Some candidates come well prepared with answers to trick questions, like "What is your greatest defect?" I avoid giving candidates the opportunity to paint unreal pictures of themselves. My questions are deliberately kept as unrelated as possible because I don't want the candidate to second-guess what I'm searching for at any given moment.

First off, I try to detect whether the person really listens to questions and understands them. It's surprising how many people don't know how to listen. If I start hearing generic answers or responses diverging from the point, I'll try a few times to simplify the questions. Once I come to the conclusion that the candidate will probably not end up working with us, I'll ease up and become friendlier, while those who answer in an interesting, pertinent way, will be kept under pressure.

I ask Mary one of my typical questions: "Is there any idea which you defend that is not mainstream in society?"

This is tricky to respond to because I'm asking the candidate to reveal an area that could very well be polemic while I don't let on what side I'm on (if I have a side).

Mary quietly ponders the question.

If Mary doesn't yet know who we are, yet puts forward something which isn't politically correct, then she's taking a risk. She might offend us, or appear as somewhat eccentric, or she could come across as extreme. Is she with a friendly or unfriendly audience? On the other hand, if she offers something mainstream, she remains on safe ground, though she'll have avoided the question. I'll be left wondering whether she understood the question, has no strong opinions or is molded by the mainstream press and equivalent sources.

Once I asked this question to a person who confidently responded with some very generic thoughts, thereby demonstrating that she hadn't understood the question, even less the pitfalls. I wondered whether it might be due to the language, so I rephrased the question, trying to explain that there could be some pitfalls and suggesting that she might like to reconsider her answer. She thanked me and responded once more in a way that was beside the point.

In her case, she did get the job although I had expressed a reservation that she didn't seem to understand questions and context. But she had a brilliant CV and we were urgently looking for somebody with her profile. Unfortunately, we had to let her go a year later, as it was too much of a struggle for her to understand our challenges and particular situation.

Mary offers her reply: "I don't believe in the education system for small children. I don't think it's a good idea to send them to school too early. Babies without their mothers for the first few months or years of life is not a good idea. If they must go to school, then the environment should be as similar to a family and a home as possible."

Now that was a daring answer, I thought. She's a young lady, who has two children and could possibly have others and is brave enough to express her opinion about raising them. She also chose an area where our mainstream system of education is sending children to school or daycare at an ever-younger age, although there's a growing, non-mainstream push for alternative education. I like her answer. It shows courage, responsibility as a parent, and awareness of current affairs.

Mary cannot tell whether I think she answered well or not. I remain emotionless and continue challenging her.

I wish to observe her levels of courage and commitment, her capacity to defend an idea, and resist stress. The interview goes on. So far my impression of Mary is rather positive, but I still wish to observe how coherent she is. Will she contradict herself? Does she measure properly the impact of what she says? This can happen with people who lie to themselves. What they think and what they think they do are sometimes at odds.

Some of the most difficult recruitments are commercial positions, people who've been trained to engage our emotions, tickle our intellect, key into our motivations, and lead us where they want us to go. They can use their skill in an interview, selling to recruiters what they want to see, and not what is in front of them.

I therefore try to hide my emotions or motivation and not give away any clues. If I can be read easily by candidates, then some will try to offer what they believe I want to hear, and thus make it difficult for me to gather a fitting opinion of the person.

On one occasion, I was asked to participate in the third interview. I encountered a brilliant salesperson, but felt

Chapter Three: The CEO in Subsidiarity

something was not quite right. My personal conclusion was that there might be trouble with him as he seemed to be hiding things. I wondered whether we would have a problem with trust and transparency. I was ready to give my feedback to the team leader, but when she finally came out of the interview she had already offered the position to the candidate. Given subsidiarity, it was her call, but he had succeeded in closing this deal before she could receive the input she had requested. This person ended up working for us for only six months. He left when we realised that he was abusing his business trips for his personal projects. Meanwhile, the team leader learned a painful lesson on recruitment.

But it also goes the other way. There was a candidate where I had strong doubts that he would adapt to the existing team. The team leader heard what I said but took the risk anyway. It was a good call as that candidate is still with us many years later and has brought new skills to the team.

We get to the end of Mary's interview. I ask her whether she thinks I had asked the right questions to form a correct opinion of who she is.

I like finishing with that type of question. The process can thus be understood. Does Mary have the capacity to analyse? What are her filters to understand this process?

Throughout my many years of interviews, there have been a number of interesting answers to this question. Sometimes the candidate will assess the questions one-by-one, going through them as if they were a laundry list. Sometimes they say "But I was expecting you to ask about my strengths and weaknesses." I'll immediately invite them to give me the answer that they had so well prepared. Some people will see the humour of this situation, others will bite their tongue, and still others will be oblivious to the irony of the situation and simply comply.

Mary responds: "I wasn't expecting those questions, but I believe they gave me the opportunity to talk about who I am. I hope I did not shock you with my answer concerning the children?"

My very last question will often be: "Do you have any questions for me? I'm the CEO of this company so perhaps there's something you would like to know?"

Often enough, I'm disappointed by the responses. I've been hiding my game during the interview, and now I'm offering a peek behind the scenes. An interview goes two ways: not only is the company looking for somebody with whom they'll be working during the upcoming years, but the person should be looking for an organisation they appreciate and that matches with their personality.

Mary starts with the typical answer: "Well, I've already asked all the questions I had in my previous interviews, so at this point I don't have any particular question". Then she pauses, and says: "I'd like to hear your own answer to one of the questions you asked me: Is there any idea which you defend that is not mainstream in society?"

I like that. She's stepped up to the challenge. And even though she's been through a stressful experience, she's able to respond.

The interview has ended. I say goodbye and walk out of the room, leaving the candidate with the team leader.

The team leader was there to look and observe. Normally, they keep silent the whole time, so as to observe the candidate more closely. Sometimes, they will need to reassure the candidate once I've gone.

A little later, the team leader and I will meet up to share our opinions. In the case of Mary, I was positively impressed. I think she'll adapt nicely. She might be a little impulsive, but she most probably will get things done.

Best practice: in the hiring process seek to evaluate whether the candidate would match up with your organisation's values

In Ian's case, he identifies what he is looking for: the person's potential for listening, understanding, and adapting to a situation along with their possibilities for adapting to the subsidiarity model, which includes the values of the common good and resilience. Ian also made the point of specifying that he will only help in the hiring process if asked: as important as this is, it falls within the realms of subsidiarity.

So in your organisation:

- *Make each manager responsible for hiring, training and providing development opportunities for the people in their area. They also need to do the firing when necessary.*
- *Transmit your interest and availability to help with the hiring process, but don't push. Remember in subsidiarity your role is one of support.*
- *When you do participate in an interview, trust that the people have the necessary skills and training. Focus on evaluating whether the person will be a good match for your organisation's values such as subsidiarity, the common good and resilience.*

The captain of the ship

The coronavirus crisis made the importance of the captain's role more evident. When everyone in the company began working from their homes, I was left wondering whether I should be doing something special.

When I need feedback or feel the need to explore ideas, I call on some members of the management team who work directly with me. We call this group "the peers", because when we get together, we're all equally free to give our opinions. They all know that I am not trying to dilute my own responsibility and that I am seeking input to feed my own decision process in my areas of responsibility. I'll make my own decisions after receiving their thoughts.

Chapter Three: The CEO in Subsidiarity

This group helps me to explore ideas and also allows the others to bounce ideas off of each other and share their challenges. They know that their issues will not be solved by anyone within the group, but being able to share them and receive some feedback can spark some new ideas, or at least help them experience that they're not alone.

So I asked this group what they thought I should do. They responded emphatically: given that we were going through turbulent times, everyone in the company needed to rely upon the captain of the ship.

Every day, therefore, I would send a message to the whole group, greeting them or sharing a thought. In addition, I live-streamed a few video presentations to explain the overall situation and gave updates as to how we were doing. I expressed confidence that the teams were well-managed, that they knew their mission and would adapt them to changing circumstances. It was important that I shared this confidence, made it known that we were heading in the right direction, and encouraged them by letting them know we were aware of what they were up to.

Since then, I've received such positive feedback about the companywide video presentations that I decided to keep them going. Many people expressed their gratitude about feeling part of the team, no matter where they were in the world.

Best practice: be attentive to communicating well to your employees

Ian offers the image of the captain of the ship who holds unto the helm in the storm. There's a special need to help keep up hope and foster unity in trying times. Like in his case, reassuring words and helpful information could be particularly welcomed and appreciated in such moments.

So in your organisation:

- Set up a group for you to be able to bounce off your ideas as regards your areas of responsibility.
- As the occasions arise, discern whether some kind of special in-company communication is needed (such as for challenging moments like epidemics).
- Invite feedback so that you can make fitting adjustments.

Conclusion

The CEO is supposed to transmit the vision of the company. In this chapter I've emphasised how our role is not so much about "doing" as it is about making sure everyone else is fulfilling their particular missions. Given that our job requires the capacity to take in realities and reflect about them, we need a certain degree of inner peace along with a setting that isn't constantly agitated by noisy activities. We ought to avoid taking on time-consuming tasks that pull us away from our mission.

Here's a list of responsibilities that should fall within our range:

- Decide upon and implement the management tools such as subsidiarity and the common good.
- Drive your key strategies, such as diversification.
- Meet regularly with your team members one-on-one, dedicating the time to give them the help they ask for and to challenge them.
- In general, challenge employees to go beyond.
- Design the work space to match your values of transparency and trust.
- Keep the pulse of the company while at the same time maintaining wide horizons.
- Watch for opportunities.
- Be available to help with recruitment, while respecting the decision of the team managers.
- In challenging times help keep the company together by transmitting an upbeat message.

Chapter Four

Closing the Loop on Subsidiarity

When I started writing this book to let other leaders of organisations know about the worth of practising subsidiarity, I didn't expect it to have a significant impact on my own employees and company. In spelling out this notion, however, I discovered how it was on everyone's lips, although some seemed to misunderstand it. One manager who reported directly to me was mistakenly blaming subsidiarity for difficulties she was having with her teams. Some in the company were struggling to apply something which was not even subsidiarity.

The Subsidiarity litmus test

To assure a general alignment amongst the employees about the concept of subsidiarity, I therefore designed the "subsidiarity litmus test", consisting of 3 questions:

1. How do you understand subsidiarity?
2. What are the advantages of subsidiarity for you and your work?
3. What are the challenges of subsidiarity?

The litmus test was run during the yearly review period in which each person takes an hour with their manager to go over their successes, failures, and hopes for the future, as well as reflect about their work and life balance. I thought it might be insightful to hear from everyone about subsidiarity, so I requested every employee to send me their answers in no more than half a page to the above three questions:

My takeaway: for some people the concept needed clarifying.

Planning a subsidiarity refresher course for the entire company

A refresher could be helpful for those who had been with us for a great many years, while a more structured explanation was needed for those who had joined us recently. Writing this book allowed me to see more clearly what subsidiarity could do if only it were understood properly.

The question was how to go about it? Should my action be restricted to the managers directly answerable to me? Or should I reach out to all the managers who work with teams? Or how about addressing the entire company?

Of course, the decision had to align with the tool of subsidiarity itself. It was in my hands to decide for my team, but I could not decide for theirs. I asked my team and they all said it would be much better for the whole company to hear about subsidiarity directly from top management.

Travel restrictions due to the Covid situation pointed towards a common video conference with all the personnel of our companies around Europe. Our training was scheduled to take place twice in the main languages spoken in our group: once in Spanish and once in French. The essential points needed to be presented in a way that wouldn't take up too much of the employees' time. In the end, I offered four one-hour sessions spread over the course of four weeks, so that people would have time to reflect about and discuss the content of each week. The content given was recorded so that those who were unable to attend could share in the experience afterwards.

Given that I had discovered that some did not realise their misunderstanding of subsidiarity, I went into the training fully aware that there could be side-effects in the company afterwards. Some of the employees were about to discover they had more power and responsibility than they thought, within their mission, and that could easily lead to friction with others who believed that they had the authority. More about this later.

The following is how I mapped out the four sessions. Note how the structure corresponds to the subsidiarity litmus test. CEOs who wish to bring subsidiarity into their companies could adapt this same content into introductory sessions for their employees.

Session 1: What is Subsidiarity?

Part I: Spelling out Key Concepts

I started this first session explaining that it fell to me as general manager to provide a management tool to organise the company. As an ice-breaker, everyone was asked to post electronically their keywords for a good management system. They came up with words like: trust, efficacy and efficiency of the organisation, bottom-up, transparency, shared energy, together, multiplying potentials, federation, learning, freedom …

Next I offered some important definitions.

Subsidiarity:

For us, subsidiarity is first of all a management tool chosen to organise a group of people so that together we can achieve something that no one person on their own could do. It's about giving the power to the people closest to the action, so they can take the decisions and apply them.

The mission defines the "What" and the "Why" but never the "How"[1].

---

[1] See pages 23—25 on the definition of the mission. For example the mission of the production manager is to make sure to have enough product in quantity and quality (that's the WHAT) to meet demand under any circumstances (that's the WHY).

Chapter Four: Closing the Loop on Subsidiarity

A person's mission needs to be negotiated between the employee and their manager. There needs to be an agreement about someone taking on a responsibility and receiving the power to carry it out.

The person who has the specific mission is not necessarily the most competent, but the one with the responsibility to carry it out. The mission has to do with a person's area of autonomy and freedom. Let me explain: the head of a department can be the best expert in a specific area, but in her mission her work is to manage a team. As team leader she will agree on a mission with one of her team members. She may very well know the optimum way forward, but by giving the mission to someone else, she will have to step back and let this other person do what they can. For the team leader it is a real challenge to give up the power and train the person while respecting their freedom and seeing the dangers. On the other hand, the mission bearer holds a real responsibility. This calls for having the wisdom to ask for guidance to the expert, while being courageous in taking the decisions.

Autonomy is the capacity to choose, within one's own mission, the best "How", at any given moment, to answer the "Why" of the mission within the "What".

Power is the ability to administer the allocated resources as chosen, and take the actions needed, without prior authorisation.

Responsibility is being accountable for successes and failures. Enjoy the success, learn from unexpected results, and benefit from or manage the consequences

Transparency is being open about what is being done and how it's happening, especially with one's own manager.

Trust is having the certainty that autonomy and power are real, even in difficult times.

Then we went over what subsidiarity is not:

- It is not a democracy. The person with the mission is the one who choses. There are no votes or negotiations.
- It is not a delegation. People are given missions, they are not delegated tasks.
- It is not the common good. Rather it's a tool that works hand in hand with the common good while remaining as something distinct.
- It is not teamwork.
- It builds on each person's quality which makes them unique.

Part II: The importance of the mission

A company should be able to create a full organisation chart that includes everyone's mission and makes clear how the company fulfils its overarching mission.

Having first delved into the nature and definition of subsidiarity, everyone then met in small group discussions for ten minutes where they shared about their own mission. They were asked to fill out a shared spreadsheet including a column for the "What" of their mission, one for the "Why" of their mission, and a column for where they would state if they had explicit assent from their manager about their mission.

During this exercise, I popped in and out of the breakout rooms, offering encouragement and witnessing the interactions between colleagues. The fact that the "What" and the "Why" columns were separated gave direction to the participants to ask the right questions. Too often the "What" is clear, but the "Why" gets forgotten.

This session was concluded by a "homework assignment": everyone was asked to go over their specific mission with their manager. Having a concise mission, in only one or two sentences, is more of a challenge than it seems.

Over the next few days, the shared spreadsheet was filled in by the participants after they had talked with their managers.

Session 2: What to expect when working in a group using subsidiarity?

I began by providing feedback about the previous session, stating that many teams had dedicated a good amount of time to exploring their missions and updating them.

Key concepts to spell out

Each person in the company has a unique talent stack, a unique combination of personality, experience and training. The objective for the company is to find the most apt mission for each person. At one and the same time, the mission will capture how they can best express their unique talents and personality, and best meet the needs of the company.

There's a need for employees to be aware of their own gifts, talents and expertise. In cooperation with their managers, they therefore need to assess their strengths and weaknesses.

Missions will be adapted to the personality of each employee. For instance some are creative but have difficulty in being persistent, while others struggle with a blank page but are great to carry things through. Others have a lot of courage to go against the flow, while some will be great in following trends and blending in. Some will have a strategic flair about foreseeing the long term consequences, while others will need to be given missions with short term implications and quick feedback.

Chapter Four: Closing the Loop on Subsidiarity

It lies within the power of the individual person **to define the "how"** of their mission, fix their own objectives and regularly discern whether their actions are aligning with their mission.

For their "how", each person has control over **their time, their training and resources: their power**. They should choose how they will organise themselves, focussing on their priorities and what will make the most impact. Then, they portion out their resources accordingly. Our company provides an internal budgeting tool which allows people to control their specific budgets by allocating (and re-allocating) resources to activities all throughout the year.

Finally, employees should keep in mind that they can count on their managers for support in carrying out their mission. Their manager is there to make sure that each person is in the right condition to carry out their mission. It's up to each person to ask for advice and guidance, to look to their manager as a sounding board, and sometimes even as someone to take on a specific task that goes beyond the person's own practical or relational capabilities.

Employees also need to **understand their responsibility**. They have to **manage their risks and recognize** what kind of mistakes are acceptable. Are they worth it? Could they be avoided? What happens if there's a mistake? In my company, for instance, risks which could affect the quality of the medicine are unacceptable, so everything should be done to avoid any errors in that area. We see the necessity to have quality control and quality assurance departments for our production and they are a requirement in our industry. In other areas, there's a greater leeway for error if it is the result of trying new ways forward. Usually, when power is widely diffused thanks to subsidiarity, individual mistakes make a limited impact on the company overall, which helps people to be more disposed to taking specific calculated risks that are important for the growth and adaptability of a company.

Individual responsibility also includes providing for **resilience** in the area of one's own mission. What could be put into place to foresee the possibility that I may not be able to come to work tomorrow? What is time dependent? What can wait? Who needs to know what I am doing in detail? Everyone should be asking and answering these questions for their own particular missions.

Responsibility means being **open to comments** from your manager, being open to suggestions, and accepting help from others.

Finally, each person should **know their teammates**, as people having strengths and weaknesses, but also as bearers of missions. They should know how all the various missions fit together, how they interact and rely upon the other. It's fundamental to have trust in the other team members, trust that each one will look after their own mission.

In reality, our missions are linked like clockwork, so this last point about how different missions fit together needed some particular attention. Some members have complementary missions, which rely heavily on others. For things to run

Chapter Four: Closing the Loop on Subsidiarity

smoothly, these individuals need to recognize the boundaries between their own mission and that of the other. They were asked, therefore, to meet in small virtual rooms in order to share their understanding of where the boundaries lay between each person's mission. The exercise included talking about the boundaries and then delineating them in a shared online page. This complex effort allowed us to observe the reality of boundaries and experience how much we need one another.

At the end of this session, it seemed as though each person were the center of the company. I therefore advised them to wait for the following week when they would understand the role of their manager and the hierarchy.

Session 3 - The Manager

Part I: A Virtual Post-it Exercise

We started the third session with each person using virtual post-its to share what they desired of their manager.

Overall, this exercise set a hopeful tone because people expressed high expectations: the manager needs to be understanding, interested, clear, humble, empathetic and much more.

The first point to cover was about the importance of the hierarchy. Who does what, and who has the responsibility for a team must be evident. This is fundamental because an organisation with a subsidiarity model is not a democracy, but rather a very clear and precise puzzle, where each mission is carried out because it's necessary and sufficient.

Part II: What the manager should do and should be.
What the manager should do

Of course managers should know their own mission.

Each manager should be well acquainted with his or her team members, so as to know how to best organise them. It's the manager who should negotiate a particular mission with each member of the crew, making sure that all the missions together are sufficient and necessary to cover his or her own particular mission. As time goes by, the manager should make sure that the missions are both understood and carried out and, furthermore, that the different missions are clicking well together. The manager should also be capable of giving needed feedback to each team member, and updating the missions when necessary.

Who the manager should be

They should have the vision for their own team; be available; appreciate the uniqueness of each person; never criticise their team, not even in private; be wary of rumours, and have a great capacity of persuasion. The manager does not impose, but knows how to explain and convince.

A manager doesn't need to be the expert of the team. In fact, being the expert might be an impediment, given that the managers will often have to sacrifice their time to allow the team members to carry out their own missions.

Good managers will challenge their team members to be sufficiently ambitious in their projects. The manager also organises regular, often monthly, one-to-one meetings to get on top of the challenges and provide an environment where projects can be explored.

We also considered the idea of the manager's manager whose mission involves helping the managers with their management challenges. This person will never intervene directly with the team and must be very careful not to undermine the manager's authority and role, but they must have an open door policy for team members who need to talk in confidentiality about their manager. This is important for avoiding silos of power (and pain).

Noteworthy in the feedback was a great interest about the manager's responsibility. This observation made for a good segue into the theme of the fourth and final week.

Session 4 - The company culture for subsidiarity to thrive

Part I: The Common good to put everything together

We put everything together in the last session. One of the risks of an organisation such as ours is that each person, or each team, can be tempted to fulfil their mission without considering their effect on others. It was time to talk about the common good and how each person, when acting, had to balance their good with the good of the group so as to maximise both. There's a need to be aware of the others and to be ready to help, as long as one's own mission is not put into jeopardy.

Part II: Group work?

I provided a questionnaire based on the three previous sessions to glean whether or not the employees thought they had learnt something useful.

The questions were as follows:

- What do you think of your level of understanding of subsidiarity before these sessions?
- How do you feel you understand subsidiarity now?
- To what extent do you feel:

    - You can apply subsidiarity to your work today?
    - Have a clear mission?
    - Have the trust of your leader?
    - Have the trust of your team members?
    - Have the trust of other departments?

- Do you feel you have enough autonomy?
- Do you feel you have too much responsibility?
- Do you feel you have the freedom to organise your time?

- Do you feel you have a clear budget?
- Do you feel you have the freedom to manage your budget?
- Are you confident that you can try out new ideas?
- Do you feel that you are transparent to your hierarchy?
- Do you feel you know enough about what the rest of your team is doing?
- Do you feel that you:

  - Have enough information to carry out your assignment?
  - Confirm your mission with your boss?
  - Would discuss subsidiarity with your colleagues again?
  - Talk with your leader about how to apply subsidiarity in your work?
- What did you get out of these sessions?

I went through the questions one by one with them, leaving time for them to write their answers. Then I shared my screen showing the amalgamation of all their answers with everyone, so we could discover together how the training sessions had gone.

The result, adjustment and the fruits

Over the next few weeks, I noted changes. Some people paid attention to the responsibility they really had, while others concentrated on their power. Many new initiatives were taken, missions were clarified and a new dynamic took root throughout the group.

Here's an example of what came about as a result of the subsidiarity training sessions. A head of department, Julia, needed to recruit a new person for her team. She understood that it was totally in her power. Her manager offered to help but she declined. A couple of weeks later, she said she had found the ideal candidate. Her manager had her doubts and asked me what to do. We told Julia that she could choose whomever she wanted, but that it might be interesting for her to see the candidate from a more detached view, with one of us conducting the interview. She accepted, knowing that she would be left free to make the choice herself. So, the next day, I carried out the interview exploring the personality of the chosen candidate. As the interview unfolded, it became evident that this person, who had a very strong academic background, had never worked in a company, did not know how to work in a team, and would really struggle to adapt to our company. I went through the interview while Julia listened carefully.

She was really shaken after the meeting because she had observed concerning aspects of the person that she hadn't realised previously. I said I would be available if she wished

Chapter Four: Closing the Loop on Subsidiarity

me to carry out an interview for the second candidate she had rejected. She thought about it and the next day organised the interview. Beforehand, I asked Julia about her doubts regarding that candidate. Julia was afraid this person would not be dedicated enough as she had abandoned her previous work for a personal project. During the interview, I explored the candidate's motivation and drive. Julia once again listened intently and came out of the interview with a totally different opinion. The next day, she announced she had changed her mind and that she would hire the second candidate. She owned the decision, while at the same time accepting that she had been mistaken, and thanking us for our help. Now, a few months later, that newly hired employee is bringing great value to the company.

Another impact of this training put stress on the company. It turned out that one of the managers wasn't fully convinced of the need for her team members to have the full responsibility for their individual missions. At the same time, those same team members realised that they could be doing more. This led to some of the team members leaving the company and, ultimately, the manager herself handing in her resignation. Having great expertise in her area, she realised that she might express her management style better somewhere else... This was painful as I have a great respect for her, but I had also witnessed the difficulties caused by the lack of alignment with subsidiarity.

My mistake was to believe that there was no major flaw in my own team, I did not want to see that there was a problem, and as a result, a branch of my organisation was suffering. When I finally saw what others had seen before me, but that I was blind to, I took the necessary steps to reorganise. It was my responsibility. I realised that I had to be vigilant and benefited from this exploration of subsidiarity.

The real touchstone for the training sessions came when I had to profoundly reorganise the entire organisation. Over time, I had taken on the direct responsibility of too many people. I needed to devote time to each of them and to grasping each person's specific challenges. As a result, I had become less and less available. I therefore reworked the organisation chart causing quite a few people to change managers. There was a risk that those who had been working directly with me, the general manager, would perceive the reorganisation as a loss of power and prestige. Thanks however to the refreshed understanding of subsidiarity, the change of manager was understood as an opportunity to receive adequate help and insights from a new manager. Trust remained in place that each would keep their autonomy, power and responsibility, even if their missions were changed.

Overall, this training put everyone on a level playing field. On the one hand, the managers knew what was expected of them, what they could do, and what they should expect. On the other hand, everyone knew the balance of power and responsibility which we strived for, and the importance of their own specific mission.

Conclusion

Even if you're still in the discernment or implementation phase of subsidiarity, keep this chapter in mind. Training sessions like the ones described here could be adapted to the phase you're in. Whether you're initiating something new or substantiating what you've already begun, remember to actively engage your employees in the process.

> **Best practises: "close the loop" by assessing and refreshing your employees' understanding of subsidiarity**
>
> *Merely speaking about our organisation's key values is not enough. It is necessary to follow up by assessing what has been understood and assimilated by the employees. It's a matter of education that requires clarifying key concepts, allowing employees the opportunity to discuss what they are learning and then following up again later. Repetition is part of learning.*
>
> *So in your organisation, when providing training about subsidiarity:*
>
> - *Make sure you yourself respect subsidiarity in the way you go about it.*
> - *Clarify key concepts such as mission (includes the WHY and the WHAT not the HOW)*

- *Spell out the roles of team managers and team members: everyone has their area of autonomy and power*
- *Highlight values such as foresight, decision, courage and empathy*
- *Be attentive to adjustments and challenges that result from the training.*

Final Conclusion

Conclusion Joan: Educating in subsidiarity

Ian knows how to employ a healthy pedagogy in his approach to implementing and reinforcing his company's fundamental management tools of subsidiarity and the common good. In other words, he knows how to walk with his employees, showing them the way, so they freely and actively avail of these tools.

Let's consider Ian's recipe for success in pedagogical terms, to zero in on some attitudes and actions that have been foundational for his type of leadership.

To begin, he was already busy during that six-month period prior to taking the helm as CEO. He started out by observing, asking questions, and listening. Ian wanted to understand firsthand the decision-making dynamics in the company. If we were using highlighters, these words would be fluorescent: invite input first. Reflect about the input you receive and take it into consideration when shaping your own views and plans.

Ian's next steps were to reach out to two people: an expert, who could corroborate his intuition about subsidiarity as the way to go; and his CFO who collaborated closely with him (and continues to do so). Here, Ian demonstrated firsthand how subsidiarity doesn't mean working alone. Like everyone else in the company, the CEO needs to take ownership of his decisions, but for that reason he relies on teamwork so he can be well informed and advised about the steps he takes. We educate best by showing how.

Another pedagogical move made early on was spelling out an organisation chart for all employees. Education includes but isn't limited to providing significant information. In this case, transmitting clear expectations is a mark of respect for others, as it sets boundaries within which they are free to act.

Once he had fully assumed his position as CEO, Ian together with Petra, accompanied the employees as they adjusted to the new way of operating. Here enters yet another element of knowing how to teach: not being afraid of repeating core concepts. I can imagine Ian had to repeat multiple times that he wouldn't be signing any purchase orders. He gives the impression that it took a while for people to register that they really did have the power to make decisions about purchases. Meanwhile he exercised his good sense of humour, patience, and kept on encouraging.

We also learn by relating what we already know to new concepts. Thus, the value of Ian's insistence that people treat their budgets at work like how they treat their home budgets; or his image of the tree to illustrate how the CEO goes on the bottom to support all the branches.

Another pedagogical measure taken by Ian is foreseeing the potential cost of mistakes made by the employees he is so constantly motivating and challenging to try new approaches. We heard from him already how taking calculated risks is linked to growth and expansion. Additionally, we learn especially well through the mistakes we make. Given that the responsibility and power is stretched out between so many employees, the system of subsidiarity can handle a certain number of individual mistakes. Ian's employees therefore know he's not going to get upset if they mess up. All this instils confidence, and most people need to feel safe to be able to take calculated risks.

We have Ian's detailed description of where he does and does not dedicate his time. He won't take on a lot of responsibilities because he wishes to invest a significant portion of his time to one-on-one meetings and to simply be available for his employees in general. Good thing because he's merely being coherent with the system he set up. Subsidiarity demands respect for the freedom of each employee. Being in a "support role" (as Ian understands it), he's aware that his greatest influence comes through personally informing, challenging, and convincing his direct reports. Since he chooses to rely on his employees to be strategic and bold in their endeavours, he's in a good position for egging them on.

Assessment and review

People learn in stages, so everything doesn't necessarily sink in right away, even if we're clear in what we say and repeat core concepts. Our personal filters can cause us to understand something quite different from what was intended by the one transmitting the idea in the first place. We also quickly forget most of what we learn, unless we practice and review it. An essential element of teaching, therefore, is assessing what you're trying to transmit and then reviewing the weak points.

Ian's "Subsidiarity Litmus Test" was a way for him to assess just how much his employees were practising subsidiarity and, then, he offered follow-up training sessions. He gets his employees actively engaged, inviting them to reflect about a question and share their answer. When people are protagonists in their own learning, they take in more. All the while, Ian himself is receiving interesting input about what his employees are understanding and where their challenges lie.

People want to feel proud of what they do. They want to contribute their ingenuity to improving something worthwhile doing. Ian's company demonstrates that it's possible for personal growth and success to be part of a greater good that includes the good of the company and the good of the customers. His management tools of subsidiarity and the common good are compatible with other kinds of companies because they match our human makeup. I hope many CEOs, and leaders of all types of organisations, will give them a try!

Conclusion Ian: It is worth it

As you arrive at the end of this book you might wonder if this management is for you and your organisation. For me it is an ongoing process. A few weeks ago, together with my

Final Conclusion

close management team, we met again with Jack, the consultant who helped us structure our thoughts around subsidiarity. This time we explored the value of virtues as management tools. How can prudence, temperance, fortitude and justice be explored and used? We honed in on practical wisdom, perseverance, magnificence, foresight, humility and justice. We toyed with the idea that the virtues are the context for each person to have guiding principles in their 'How' as they carry out their missions. One feedback Jack gave us and which stuck with me is that he expects us to be around for a long time. Many companies fail in times of uncertainty, but with our organisation, resilience is built in our DNA. We have the creativity, culture and environment which allow us to reshape and reinvent ourselves on a regular and organic level. Every person in the company is constantly tweaking their processes to adapt and deliver.

Our organisation in subsidiarity has been a great opportunity to see the skills of many people blossom and bear fruit. I have been continuously surprised and impressed by the creativity and grit of people all through the company.

I can only encourage you to take the risk of trying to work with subsidiarity, whether in your families, your associations, your companies and any organisation, where you try to inspire others to participate in a worthwhile mission. I hope this book might help you.

www.ingramcontent.com/pod-product-compliance
Lightning Source LLC
LaVergne TN
LVHW020931090426
835512LV00020B/3308